EMOTIONALLY TRUMPED OUT

EMOTIONALLY TRUMPED OUT

So You're Outraged, Now What?

Diane Altomare

FIRST EDITION

Author Photograph by Stacey Crnich

Library of Congress Cataloging-in-Publication Data has been
applied for.

ISBN 978-1-7327274-0-3

This book was written to honor our freedom of speech, one of the freedoms I hold dear. I simply can't imagine life without personal expression.

And to every journalist, that has dedicated their life to protecting our freedom of speech and our democracy by holding our leaders accountable ... I, along with many Americans, are eternally grateful.

CONTENTS

"Regardless of where you stand on the issues, name calling and labeling from any part of the political spectrum is harmful to our national health. We must find common ground in order to work for solutions for our kids' tomorrows. Diane Altomare powerfully illustrates how to resist the urge to react and to instead choose clarity, strength and the courage to pause, consider, and respond effectively. The peace and security of our country, for which I and my family have paid so high a price, depends upon each of us heeding Diane's insight and guidance."

-ROB DUBOIS,
retired Navy SEAL, founder of the High Impact Mindset, and author of *Powerful Peace: Lessons on Peace from a Lifetime at War*

"Emotions are running high and the chasm is growing even wider. It's normal to feel everything from anxiety to rage to helplessness. Don't despair. The moment you come into connection with any of these emotions, herein these pages, you will find powerful wisdom to help you transcend the very emotion, conversation or relationship that's upsetting you. This timely wisdom and guidance will catapult you to the other side, where peace, love and harmony reside."

-DONNA LIPMAN,
co-founder of Lumen Worldwide and author of
Beyond Resistance

"The emotional outbursts and immaturity present within the current political landscape, are a symptom of people not being taught emotional intelligence. This illuminating guide contains nuggets of wisdom to process through whatever you're feeling about all that's taking place and usher you to a place of more peace and less fear, anger or anxiety."

-BETSY CHASSE,
award winning filmmaker of What The Bleep Do We Know, and author of *Dancing In The Unknown*

THE DIVIDE

It's hard to imagine the divide in this country being any wider than it is today. However, the possibility that we become even more polarized is looming, as we continue to be inundated with new allegations, breaking news and issues to process through every day in this country.

The deeper I have dove into conversations with people on both sides about the issues we're facing, the more the political opinions and reasons for emotional upset seem to starkly contrast one another. And the more difficult it seems to see each other's point of view. There is one thing plainly obvious, however, that both sides have in common:

We are fighting against each other instead of facing these issues together.

So what's going on? As complex as much of this

may seem to be, at a very simple and basic human level, there is one answer to the collective emotional battle we are engaging in on a daily basis in this country: *we are at war with not only each other, but ourselves.* And many of us are playing out our wounds, flinging them haphazardly into the political chaos. In many cases, instead of dealing with the emotional upset we feel, we are projecting it onto each other causing more hatred and division.

I do realize that only five paragraphs into this book, you may be ready to put it down, wondering how in the world the division in our country has anything to do with what's going on within you personally. But stay with me. Because it does.

And I promise to show you exactly why this may be the very insight, wisdom and understanding you are craving at a deep soul level.

I also must say, right here on page two before I start talking about President Trump and the emotional upheaval he has awakened that this book isn't about making Trump the villain, although some may want to make that case. More importantly, what is going on emotionally in this country is about you. And it's about me. It's inclusively, about all of us. Trump is simply the catalyst that has awakened what has been suppressed within and simmering beneath the surface in our lives, for many years.

So here's how this works. I was bullied when I was younger and there's a wound there. Much of it has been healed through the inner work I've done over the past two decades, however I still have a sensitivity to being bullied or watching others be bullied.

So what happens when I feel Trump, or anyone else, bullying someone? I get angry, upset and feel compelled to call it out. I am affected by it; highly sensitive to it. And in that moment, because I'm being affected, I know it is my shadow self coming to the surface. And more significantly, the emotional upset is showing me that there's more work to do to heal this part of me that felt bullied, attacked and shamed when I was younger.

So imagine our country, collectively vulnerable, to each of our individual wounds; these unresolved emotional upsets or traumatic events from the past, swirling around within us, with no place to go. Except for that moment, when they are poked at by the emotional intensity in our country and in a split second projected outward onto something or someone that has triggered those wounds.

From this vantage point, it becomes crystal clear why there's so much emotional upheaval and why many of us are emotionally responding to and sometimes being wildly thrown all over the place by the Trump presidency, the media's coverage of this administration and all the other Americans around us reacting to what's happening, at moments, from their wounded selves.

To make things even more complicated, not only are each of our individual shadows being revealed, but our collective shadows as a country are being played out as well.

The shadow, psychologist Carl Jung described, is any part of us that we don't want to be. And so we hide it, push it away and suppress it. We all have many shadows; many aspects or qualities we don't want to possess. It's simply part of being human.

Your shadow may be revealing itself right now, as someone on social media labels you a bully, arrogant, sensitive, racist, weak, sexist, a snowflake, angry, mean or hateful, and it puts you on the defensive. Your shadow is any quality, you see being played out in this intense political climate that gets you fired up or makes you reactive.

It's simple to identify your shadows. Just notice, where you get upset, angry, frustrated or feel an intense emotional reaction and you will be revealing one of your wounds, a shadow part of you that has been hidden and needs to be healed.

Unfortunately, when we are affected by something someone says on social media or at the dinner table, many of us don't take the time to reflect on how we are feeling or process through our emotional upset before responding. Instead, we may react emotionally with a nasty tweet or hostile post. Precisely, why these are plentiful on social media.

Our challenge is to change this national battle into an internal healing, so we can come to these issues with grounded, clear intentional focus, instead of emotional chaos. This is not always easy to do because your shadows and unresolved emotions, have been hidden within you and each has powerful energy driving you, often compelling you to express yourself immediately, intensely, and reactively.

The anger you may be spewing at your spouse for disagreeing with you on building the wall is absolutely understandable. Yes, it's valid. And I know you have a reason, just as I and many others, to feel angry about this injustice, regardless of whether you feel we should build the wall or not. But the depth of that anger isn't just about the wall or immigration or racism, it's also about what's going on within you. It's about the anger you may have suppressed within yourself and haven't known what to do with.

And then along comes Donald J. Trump, the 45th

president of the United States to stir up our emotional upset and bring it to the surface, as we collectively react and project it into a national debate and emotional war.

The difficulty many of us are facing with all this emotional upset being unleashed, is we don't have the tools to process through it or if we do, we simply aren't using them. It doesn't matter how angry or upset we get about any of the issues facing our country, until we process through our anger and other emotions in a healthy way, we can't and won't be part of the solution.

We will just be another face of one of the many hateful and vicious comments to be posted on social media.

And herein lies the moment of choice. We are each being given a huge gift: a spiritual awakening, a lifelong healing and the opportunity for a whole new evolution and emergence of both our individual self and our collective self as a country, to rise up and evolve.

So are we up to this huge undertaking? I posed this question to my friends on social media. The question I asked is:

"Do you believe it is possible to heal the divide in our country?"

And here's what some said:

"I don't know where to begin, but I hope so."

"It looks like no, sadly. But somehow, someway love must prevail. The divide is so big."

"Yes. But it has to start with who we are electing to local politics."

"My teachers' teacher answered this question the following way: when mankind becomes KindMan. KindWoman."

"Yes, I do. But it takes those of us who believe it, to stop the divide in its tracks. Refuse to engage in the hate."

"When we have leaders at the top that know how to be leaders, this can all start to change quite quickly. Right now we need that more than ever before."

"Absolutely not until the idiot is out of office."

"Absolutely yes! Politics is a pendulum swing. This too shall pass, but there is an awful lot of water under the bridge and a lot of damage to undo."

"No."

"Yes, presidents will come and go...we need to focus on how we are alike rather than all of our differences...And be respectful of one another."

"We can differ, we can hate that we differ, we can run away from our differences, but on a round planet there are no sides. We're in this together."

"I don't know. As I see being healed deeply in some places. But at the same time, it is like asking if hunger and poverty will ever end."

"Not until law and order is back. This election has changed many people. I don't think anyone will be able to relax again. I think Americans will now be engaged in politics from now on."

And this final response to the question I posed, is what this book is all about.

"Of course. But it needs to begin at the soul level."

So before we dive into this soul level healing, here's a bit of caution about what's to come.

Some of what I say, may be in complete opposition to what you believe, politically or otherwise. And you may be triggered by what I write, the way I write, what I'm trying to communicate or the political views I hold.

And I ask as a part of our emotional healing, that you extend me some grace, especially in the moments you get triggered by what I'm saying. And instead of putting the book down and labeling me one way or the other, that you press on, so that ultimately we can come together and see the places where we are connected and hold common ground, instead of those where we differ. And more importantly, you use the places where you feel triggered to dive deeply into your unresolved emotions, your shadow self, the places where you are wounded and places where you have the opportunity to heal.

I have been doing this inner reflection and shadow work for the past two decades and have coached many others to do this work, as well. And I have consciously chosen to intently focus on even more of my own healing and embracing of shadows, throughout the writing of this book. I have had the opportunity and humbling experience of being triggered and affected by many of you that hold widely differing political views than I, as we've talked through these issues together. And although it hasn't been easy to have these conversations, it's been worth it and personally healing. Here's what I shared on social media, early on in the writing of this manuscript.

My thoughts on day 28: This is not an easy book to write in this divisive time. Not because the words aren't coming to me, because they are. But because there are so many things I must say, that will offend somebody...because we're all so divided on so many different issues.

I am feeling the heaviness of it all today. I know that some of what I will write will have some people unfriend and unfollow me, and it is a risk that I am going to have to take.

Because there are things that I must say and that I feel compelled to share. My intention isn't to offend or cause any more division. And that is the irony here.

My intention truly is to express what I see happening and to shine a light onto much of the darkness and the ways that we are each a part of this divisive time. The ways we are each choosing to judge one another, albeit often unconscious.

This isn't an easy process, but it is worth it. And it is necessary.

I hope you will join me on this journey and

give me, yourself and others grace, as we work through reconnecting to each other, one conversation and one heart connection at a time.

As I share this previous post with you, I truly feel it is the crux of this whole book and the inner reflection, you will hopefully find yourself doing:

To extend grace, as we work through reconnecting to each other, one conversation and one heart connection at a time.

It is this very grace and compassion, you will want to give yourself as well, as you dive inward and reflect on what the emotional upheaval is mirroring for you and how it has been disconnecting you from peace, happiness, what you want in your life and even the people you love.

THE GIFT OF TRANSFORMING YOUR EMOTIONS

We are emotional beings. Not one day passes in our life without each of us feeling something. It doesn't matter what it is, all feelings are valid. What is most important, is that you honor your emotions and acknowledge that they are powerful messengers.

Each one here, to help you individually expand and evolve; to help us collectively grow and change. This is a time like no other, where we are being called to become conscious of the emotional upset within each of us and use it as an opportunity to heal, instead of getting mired in the chaos of it all.

There is a big difference between being consumed by an emotion or using it as a catalyst to make a difference; allowing it to render you powerless or fueling your courage to take a stand.

One is allowing the emotion to run rampant and control you. The other is consciously processing through the emotion and gaining the insight it holds; using the energy of it to take peaceful, transformative action.

Here's an example. You see something on the news and it enrages you; it fires you up, as you scream obscenities at the TV. Anybody have that experience lately? And you allow it to control you and consume you. You allow that negative energy to swirl within your body— that anger or upset to simmer within you all day, making you a bit irritable or even somewhat down.

Here is another option. You instead, consciously choose to use the energy of that emotion as a catalyst to take action, that's aligned with what you want to create more of. This conscious decision will create quite a different experience.

You see that same news event and it still enrages you. You may still shout at the TV. But here's the difference. After you are done yelling at your TV screen, you consciously choose to connect deeply with the feeling of that emotion, process it in a healthy way and get the anger, outrage and upset out of your body. By doing this, you connect with and understand what that anger or upset is trying to communicate to you.

Maybe the voice of your anger is saying, "This isn't ok," or "I have to do something to be a part of the solution." You connect deeply with the voice of this emotion and you acknowledge your ability to take action.

As a result, maybe you rally people together, speak your truth, bring love and light to everything you do that day or you have more courage to bring your unique gift, knowing the world is in desperate need of what you offer.

So you go out that day with more courage than you ever thought you had, knowing that now is the time to step up in your life, speak out more in your community and bring more of who you are to everything you do. This option, obviously, is the more empowering one and is how we can each make a difference, despite this challenging time in history.

This option is the one that led many to march and start the women's movement. And it is the same empowering choice that is driving many people who haven't run for office before, to get in the game and make things different.

THE GIFT OF THIS EMOTIONAL UPHEAVAL

In order to approach our life with this more empowering option, we have to understand what's happening emotionally both within ourselves and with the nation, as a whole.

Trump is a master at stirring up peoples' emotions. And to be frank, it doesn't matter what political side you're on. This president emotionally stirs things up and you are left with choosing who you are and what you are going to do with how you feel. Your job is simply to be conscious of what emotions have awoken and respond in a way that transforms the situation. By doing that, you will be using this emotional awakening as the healing, it's intended to be.

Emotional upheaval is happening on both sides and on most issues and is part of what's causing the division and turmoil in this country. But it doesn't have to continue, if we are willing to bring consciousness to what's truly going on and declare to choose a more empowering, transformative option.

This post, where I called out President Trump for his name calling, labeling and bullying, went off the rails and awry many times with people attacking each other, calling each other names, and obvious emotional projection and division present. On a personal note, I was attacked quite a few times for calling the president out on his behavior. It occurred over a few days, with 300 plus comments, many intensely heated. But in the end, some hearts were softened, hot buttons were diminished, people embraced their projections and we learned a lot from our experience together. Here's a few examples of how opposed both sides were:

1ST SOCIAL MEDIA THREAD

Scott: I believe that the divide between Constitutional originalists and Progressives is deep, wide and unbridgeable but once people get clear on where they stand we can be kind, generous, and loving while we work to advance our chosen philosophies. An ideology isn't the same as a person; attack the ideology and not the person.

Karen: Better idea...Let's stop attacking altogether.

Scott: Karen, how about you deal with your side on that.

When Google lists "Nazism" as part of the ideology of the California GOP, isn't that an attack? Are you saying that when conservatives defend themselves they are attacking? If you don't see your own attacks you will think that the defense of others is an attack on you; that they initiated the altercation.

A 12-step principal is take your own inventory and maybe if we all looked in the mirror a little more, we would have less time to see what everybody else is doing? Sweep on your side of the street first.

Scott: Karen with all due respect your request indicates that you don't really understand the issues that separate us. Should you wish to become informed you can read many books to learn how the other side thinks and why there's such opposition to leftism by conservatives.

Karen: It is not necessary that I understand the issues in the same way that you understand them. Please do not tell me that I am uninformed or try to control me with "facts" from your arsenal. This is insulting, which is the point to this exercise. This was all about getting better at respectfully acknowledging the opinions and ideologies that others hold without attacking, belittling or insulting them in the process.

Scott: Karen, whether or not you're uninformed is a matter of fact, that's not an opinion. I can only guess at whether or not you are uninformed, there's no way for me to know this for certain. To me, you sound uninformed about the issues separating us but I could be wrong. You certainly are defensive about it. That's observable fact.

Karen: Scott, once again your comments above are arrogant and insulting at best. It is not OK to disrespect others just because they don't believe the same things you believe.

Scott: Karen, if you'd like to retract your unfounded accusation, this would be an appropriate time to do so.

You can feel the tension in this interaction. And from this place where people are made wrong for their view, healing, understanding and compassion is challenging. However, the very fact that both people are willing to have this conversation is progress. And therein lies hope. Because as I will share more about in a moment, what I learned from this post and the 300 plus comments that were left, is that people do want to work through this. From a deep place, most of us want to heal this division.

2ND SOCIAL MEDIA THREAD

Rachel: The minute Trump made fun of a disabled man, made me vomit and I can't believe people can look at this and be ok with it.

Cindy: Stop listening to fake news! You are being brainwashed.

Rachel: No, I'm not. I saw the whole thing, full context. All the words. He is a mean man. It's not fake news. I'm not arguing. But in your words, I'm calling "rotten" rotten, that's just the truth and there is no love without truth.

Laura: no one is perfect

Diane Altomare: Policies do not justify his disgraceful behavior. I lovingly disagree with you Laura. Saying "he isn't perfect" isn't enough and still doesn't make it ok.

Rachel: I am a physical therapist. I'm very

aware of the different diagnoses. I'm certain Trump is not. Even though Trump lied and said he didn't know this guy, I tend to believe the guy who said Trump did know him, even by name. He covered him for years. My point being, the upper extremity flexed posture that this man presents is a common flexed posture seen with various neurological conditions. Yes his joints are fixed, but Trump's flailing motions are representative of a spastic disorder that I'm certain he was putting on this young man. Trump has no idea the difference between various neurological conditions...completely inappropriate and uncalled for.

Diane Altomare: And truly, there is no reason to dispute just this one mention of Trump making fun of people. He does it often with his mean comments, name calling and labeling. It's truly a waste of energy to refute this one moment in Trump's long list of ugly comments toward people. My question is, "how can people turn away from how he treats people so inhumanely just because they like his policies?"

Laura: We all make fun of people.

Tammy: uuhhh...no I don't.

3RD SOCIAL MEDIA THREAD

Karen: Trump is the poorest excuse for a role model for our young generation that our country has ever seen. His fascist leadership style is endangering our country. I can't understand why anyone would like this man. He has done nothing for this country except pass a tax law that drains the poor and elderly and gives it to the top 10%. Fake news? Russian money laundering? Defunding women's healthcare? Cutting veterans benefits? Demonizing immigrants? Admitted affairs with porn stars? Cozying up to the NRA while our school kids are being shot and killed? Obstruction of justice? Bleeding his presidency for his family's financial gain? Antagonizing unstable dictators with nuclear capabilities? I can go on and on. Why is this OK?

Diane, I am completely in agreement with you about his behavior and can't wait to see this horrible man impeached or removed from office. We all deserve better. Brighter days are ahead after midterm elections. Mueller is bringing him down.

Scott: There goes the calm, thoughtful and rational discussion. Don't wonder any longer why political discussions go off the rails.

Karen: Scott, of course it's nothing personal...Just opinions. Isn't this the whole point of discussion?

Scott: Karen, I believe if you were to speak about the issues instead of attacking the person you'd get more agreement, perhaps even from Pres. Trump himself, should you ever have an opportunity to talk to him directly. Your statement was full of inaccuracies and vitriol which makes having a dialogue with those who don't share your opinions more than a little bit difficult.

Before we continue on with this social media thread, right here is why we need to process through our emotions and embrace our shadows before continuing on, in conversations like these. Because people are going to trigger us; they are going to hit our hot buttons in the language they use. And it is our individual responsibility to process through how we're feeling first, so we can come back to the conversation without being affected or heated and effectively communicate how we feel. This is how you empower yourself and heal, while at the same time, healing the emotional divide.

Karen: Scott, there is no attacking going on. I am simply stating my opinions just as you are. The mistake we tend to make is assuming personal attack when differences are expressed.

Scott: Karen, "poorest excuse for a role model, fascist leadership style, money laundering, defunding women's healthcare, demonizing immigrants, admitted affairs with porn stars, obstruction of justice." These allegations are smears and unproven accusations which you pass along as fact. That you would take as fact the word of the porn star/actress and her disreputable attorney over that of the Pres. regarding the alleged affair puts you in the camp of those who would turn our system of justice upside down – guilty until proven innocent.

If you don't often have dialogue with those who don't see things in the same way as you, my objection to your language and style may be surprising to you. The lens through which we observe the same facts makes the world we live in appear very different. I'll do my best to understand what you are seeing and hear your passion, even though it comes in harsh inaccurate rhetoric.

Karen: Scott, I respect your right to express your opinion. You will never change my mind. This is not a debate platform but rather a tool for learning how to get along with others who have a differing opinion than yours.

In this interaction, some healing took place and one of the parties was able to accept the disagreement and not be affected or triggered by it any longer. Here's what she shared:

Karen: Diane, I feel as though my process has come full circle. This post was extremely helpful. After witnessing all of this debating and character slandering, in the end, my reaction buttons have dissolved. Thank you for all of your dedication and hard work on this.

Insight About Social Media Interaction

As you witnessed from these different social media threads, so many raw emotions were being felt and projected here. I heard from many people who contributed to this post, privately as well. People were being triggered and affected intensely, which is obviously exactly what has been happening in this intense political climate in our country.

This post was simply a microcosm of the macrocosm. And as I shared often throughout this conversation, healing the emotional divide is not about trying to get the other side to see your point of view or ultimately, even agree with you. It is about each one of us being heard, and more importantly, doing the inner work to heal our wounds when we are being triggered or affected by what somebody does or says. That is the opportunity we each have and it's a huge gift, if we are willing to turn inward and do the inner work needed, instead of projecting our victimhood, anger, hatred, fear and anxiety outward onto others.

What I personally took away from the many different threads on the post, was that even though many people were rigidly holding onto their point view and had to be right at all costs, that at a deep level most of us want to figure out how to change this. We want to reconnect to each other, we want to understand each other and we want to be heard. And in that, lies HOPE. Hope that we can and will heal this emotional divide.

Here is a powerful way to visualize what occurred in this post and bring with you, as a reminder, when you are being triggered or affected in your conversations with others.

Internationally renowned NY times best-selling author Dr. Wayne Dyer, said squeeze an orange and what comes out? Orange juice.

Dyer goes on to say, "When someone squeezes you, puts pressure on you, says something you don't like, offends you. And out of you comes anger, hatred, bitterness, fear. It's because that's what's inside."

"It's one of the great lessons of life," Dr Dyer says. "It doesn't matter who does the squeezing—your mother, your brother, your children, your boss, the government. If someone says something about you that you don't like, what comes out of you is what's inside."

LEADING BY EMOTIONAL REACTION

When Donald Trump is criticized or questioned, he often retaliates, going for the jugular with mean, hateful comments. In one of his many incendiary tweets, he says: "The @WSJ Wall Street Journal loves to write badly about me. They better be careful or I will unleash big time on them. Look forward to it!"

The tweets and comments are many. "I never watch Don Lemon, who I once called the dumbest man on television," Trump tweeted. He repeatedly calls Senator Warren, "Pochahontas" and said at a campaign rally in Virginia, "Pocahontas is not happy, she's not happy. She's the worst. You know, Pocahontas — I'm doing such a disservice to Pocahontas, it's so unfair to Pocahontas — but this Elizabeth Warren, I call her 'goofy,' Elizabeth Warren, she's one of the worst senators in the entire United States Senate."

And here's a tweet, where the president is attacking Morning Joe co-host Mika Brzezinski and Joe Scarborough, "I heard poorly rated @MorningJoe speaks badly of me (don't watch anymore)," Trump said in a pair of tweets. "Then how come low I.Q. Crazy Mika, along with Psycho Joe, came to Mar-a-Lago 3 nights in a row around New Year's Eve, and insisted on joining me. She was bleeding badly from a face-lift. I said no!"

And we can't forget the tweet, the president aimed at Senator Gillibrand, "Lightweight Senator Kirsten Gillibrand, someone who would come to my office "begging" for campaign contributions (and would do anything for them)."

It is in those moments when you realize you're being triggered or affected by his tweets, for example, that you must resist the urge to immediately take your emotions to social media and instead, go within. Resist the knee jerk reaction to react emotionally, fueling the fire of division and hatred, and instead tend to your emotional upset. In that moment, your job is to acknowledge how you are feeling and why. And then give that emotion a voice, so you understand it's purpose and message.

So why does the President of the United States, a man who seems to have it all, call people names and stoop to such childish playground tactics? Because that's what's within him. The shadow of insecurity, anger, and hostility are swirling inside the president and haven't been acknowledged, processed or released in a healthy way. And then when he is criticized or "squeezed" as Dr. Wayne Dyer says, "what comes out, is what's inside."

Of course, these are some of the same emotions that have been suppressed and are swirling inside each one of us. If unattended to and not processed consciously and intentionally, these emotions build up within waiting for that moment of pressure and then they explode; without a moment's notice, and often inappropriately and disproportionately.

In the next chapter, we will dive deeply into one

of the emotions that has been suppressed within so many of us and is being projected outward into our collective conversations, at an alarming rate. And that's, *anger*.

TRANSFORMING ANGER

There's a lot to be angry about. Check out any social media conversation, listen to the pundits debating on TV or strike up a conversation with somebody you disagree with politically, and most likely you will either connect to your own anger or at some point in the conversation, witness somebody else getting angry.

Now multiply that by approximately 300 million people in the United States of America, projecting their anger onto each other, in response to what's happening politically. And it's no wonder why there is so much explosive energy, right now.

Anger can be both damaging and toxic when projected onto someone else or suppressed within.

Here are a couple examples of anger being

unleashed onto another in the political conversations, we've been having on social media:

> "Hey Moron, there's no secret that I'm a conservative.
> We all have to weigh and use our judgment on anything we read or watch. But, you have to have judgment to use when you're doing that. I'm not clear that you have any and you aren't displaying much in this conversation."

> "The person standing beside me could be a Trump supporter and I say "they can go to hell." I have my right to my beliefs and believe if you believe in Trump you're an idiot and are heartless. You can all go to Hell."

Given how palpable the anger is in the many hostile comments on social media and political conversations lately, you may be wondering whether it's detrimental to our well-being to have this much intense, explosive outrage in our country right now. And the answer is yes, hands down; it's definitely detrimental, both individually and as a country.

However, there is a silver lining; a light to all this darkness, if we are willing to acknowledge it. Anger is a huge mobilizer and can be a powerful transformative energy when utilized in a positive and intentional way; when used for change, when funneled into something positive.

In a few moments, we will be exploring that in detail. But before we dive into how to use your anger, as fuel for positive change, let's stop for a moment and identify your relationship with anger.

Here is a simple, but revealing question to ask yourself, to determine your level of comfort with anger:

"Am I ok with being angry, or is anger an emotion I tend to avoid at all costs?"

Anger often gets a bad rap, because it's an explosive emotion, both to experience in oneself and to witness someone else express. And anger, can of course be frightening, when unleashed in a violent or abusive way.

However, being angry is a healthy response when your values are being violated or what you deem acceptable in society, is no longer what's happening. There is much that has awakened my anger throughout the Trump Presidency. Such as the president calling people names and stirring up hate at his rallies, the hateful rhetoric on social media becoming common place, Trump's hostility towards the media and this administration separating children from their parents at the border, to name just a few.

One of the ways I have used the energy of my anger as fuel for positive change, is to express how I feel and call out the injustices I see. That is exactly what I did in this post, where I called out the president for his divisive nature; for pitting one side against the other. Why would I do this? Very simply and significantly to shine a light on his dark, demeaning, destructive behavior. Behavior, that I find morally and societally reprehensible from any one and even more so, from the President of the United States.

As you will see, people got angry at me for doing this. And in some instances, instead of respectfully disagreeing with my view, a few people directed their anger at me and attacked me personally. Which ironically, is exactly what I was calling out the president for doing.

MY POST

News flash, Mr. President: you were hired to represent all of America, not pit one side against the other.

"Democrats want anarchy, they really do, and

they don't know who they're playing with, folks," says Donald Trump, at his rally in Montana, last night.

You're kidding, right Mr. President? Threatening democrats (half the country). This is how you make America Great again? No, this is how you pit one side against the other, like a bully on a playground. Disgraceful!

SOCIAL MEDIA THREAD

Brenda: Children, teens and adults learn from everyone. What are they learning from this president?

Diane Altomare: Great question Brenda! That is a question we must each ask ourselves. "What am I learning from this president and is it aligned with my deepest truth?"

Kristy: You say you're a coach, but your comments create division. You're really a hypocrite and a fraud . . . the way you're bashing our President is a disgrace. Maybe, your next book should be about hypocrisy.

Diane Altomare: My calling this president out for his disgraceful behavior is completely in alignment with who I am, what I value and stand for.

Thank you for sharing your thoughts, however it is not necessary to insult me Kristy...that is what this president teaches daily. Regardless of that, I honor and respect how you feel!

Lara: I agree Kristy. President Trump has been one of the best presidents ever! The divide started with Obama. People just don't like Trump because he 'tells it like it is' and they can't handle it.

Kristy: I agree Lara and love Trump. He's not a politician and he's definitely keeping his promises. And to Diane, you can't say you want to heal the divide and at the same time, say such angry things about the President, which just creates more division. It's like pouring salt on a wound.

Diane Altomare: I am not creating more division. I am asking you to allow me to have my views, as I respect your views. We can still be friends and not attack each other or shame each other. That is how to heal the emotional divide: to learn how to process through our own individual emotions and not project our upset onto each other. My anger for the way this president treats and disregards women, among many other things, was not directed at you. Your emotional upset, directed at me, is what I am working to help people to stop doing. And that is how we will heal this emotional divide. Thank you for being a part of this conversation!

Diane Altomare: Kristy, anger is a healthy emotion, it's part of being human and when expressed properly, can fuel positive change. Anger often signals that something we believe in or that is important to us, is being violated. It's not like pouring salt on a wound. It's simply an emotional expert, expressing her anger, in a healthy way and emulating the way to stand up for what she believes in.

Kristy: Healthy anger? Spare me. Anger is negative and not helpful at all. How is this possibly helping to heal the emotional divide?

Linda: I'm angry at the way he disrespects women too. But not just women. He ridicules and name-calls everyone – even members of his own party and cabinet. Except when it comes to Putin.

I'm also angry that our president is teaching our children and all who watch him on television or follow him on twitter – that it's okay to be mean, nasty, name-call and bully – there's a difference between "telling it like it is" and encouraging name-calling and disrespect.

It makes me sad, after decades of leaders speaking out against bullying, school programs and after school programs teaching children to be nice to each other – that we have a president who comes along and destroys all of that hard work.

Lara: Kristy, I agree with you! This post, bashing our president creates more of a divide.

Linda: I find it interesting that you ladies love Trump because "he tells it like it is" – yet Diane's post "tells it like it is" by literally posting a recent quote from Trump himself – and you call her divisive?

How is that possible? She's just telling it like it is, right?

Cathy: Linda, perfect point!

Diane Altomare: Kristy, I have been working to heal the emotional divide for months now, and I am absolutely seeing people on both sides stop projecting their anger, fear and upset onto each other and have civil conversations here on this page, even though so many of us strongly disagree with each other and these are tough, emotional conversations to have.

Tim: You do state a truth, Lara. The right began their divisiveness during President Obama's terms. I never stated that Trump is not our president. He is however, by far, even half way through his term, the worst in American History. Can you elaborate on what you mean by, telling it like it is?

Tim: Kristy, do you not really see what is going on?

Tim: Linda yes! Lara and Kristy do not get that part.

Cathy: These ladies flatly refuse to look at any real facts or opinions other than their own. Even though many of their "facts" are actually inaccurate. Why do they feel safe living in half truths?

Linda: Cathy, I would venture to guess, because so far they nor anyone close to them has been directly affected or in the line of fire. It's a sad reality these days.

Many of us have been a part of conversations like this or have witnessed this kind of projection, taking place.

Here's our challenge, in moments like this: to resist the urge to either attack or shut down and instead process through our emotions, so we emerge stronger and more whole. In short, instead of directing our upset towards others like we saw at moments in the post above, we must process through how we are feeling first, and in addition, use it as an opportunity to embrace our shadows and heal.

Every time I was insulted, or felt triggered or affected by what somebody was saying, I processed through my emotions and embraced a new shadow.

Ultimately, I used peoples' projections and upset to become stronger and more empowered, instead of getting defensive and attacking them in return. This is the opportunity we each have. To use our emotional upset, as the awakening it's intended to be. It is not always easy to do but is how we can use these challenging times to grow and evolve, instead of allowing our differences to weaken our emotional state.

EMBRACING YOUR SHADOWS

Unfortunately for many of us, projection is all too common these days. Many of us have been insulted or called derogatory names by someone who disagrees with us politically.

People often resort to name calling because they are intensely emotional and don't know what to do with how they feel. So instead of allowing themselves to feel angry or frustrated, they hurl an insult at you or call you a name to relieve the intensity they're feeling. If you are affected by the name or insult, therein lies an opportunity to embrace one of your shadows and emerge stronger.

As Debbie Ford, groundbreaking leader on the shadow taught: "Our shadow contains all the parts of ourselves that we have tried to hide or deny, the parts we believe are not acceptable. It is made up of everything that annoys, horrifies or disgusts us about other people or about ourselves. It holds all that we try to hide from those we love and all that we don't want other people to think about us or find out about us. It dictates our attractions and our repulsions and determines what we will love and what we will judge and criticize."

There are many shadows being played out right now in our political climate. Simply write a list of all the derogatory names you've heard people being called and you will be identifying some of the shadows, once suppressed, that are now acting out.

Let's identify a few: hypocrite, bully, arrogant, brainwashed, sensitive, racist, weak, sexist, a snowflake, mean, heartless and the list goes on and on.

Let's say someone calls you a snowflake and sarcastically directs you to go to your safe space. By labeling you a snowflake, what they may be implying is that you are either too sensitive or too weak to handle a conversation with them. Because they are in judgment of your sensitivity or weakness, we know that "weak" is one of their shadows. In other words, they can't allow themselves to display "weakness" in their life. So instead, they project or transfer their disdain for "being weak," onto you.

Remember all the crafty little names, Donald Trump has come up with? Here's a short list of some of the names, he has called people he doesn't like:

- *Crooked Hillary*
- *Low IQ Maxine Waters*
- *Little Marco*
- *Crazy Joe Biden*
- *Lying James Comey*
- *Lightweight Senator Gillibrand*
- *Cheatin' Obama*
- *Little Adam Schiff*
- *Cryin' Chuck Schumer*
- *Goofy Elizabeth Warren*
- *The Dumbest Man On Television Don*
- *Crazy Low IQ Mika*

One could rightfully argue that each one of these names is one of Donald Trump's shadows; a quality or aspect he doesn't want to be. So instead, he projects it onto someone else. He deflects attention from his own shadows and uses them to make someone else feel small or weak, in an attempt to feel or appear mighty and powerful. However, like a bully on a playground in elementary school, his shadows are still in plain sight even though he is desperately trying to cover them up.

Unfortunately, there are many people on social media that have followed the president's lead. We have all seen heavy doses of name calling and bullying. I myself have been called; a hypocrite, stupid, annoyingly pompous, a warmonger, weak and sensitive, to name just a few.

Remember, when we call each other names, what we are doing is attempting to shame each other. It's a way people will attempt to bully you or try to put you in your so-called "place." Often their attempt to silence you is because they can't deal with what you're saying, are being emotionally affected by it or don't know how to respond to your comment or view in a civil or compassionate way.

But the brilliance of shadow work, is both simple and profound. If you embrace both your dark and light shadows, for example, stupid and it's polar opposite smart, you emerge more whole and less affected by someone trying to shame you or attack you. You are then empowered to communicate in a clear, effective way.

As Debbie Ford states, in *The Dark Side of the Light Chasers*, "Our shadows exist to teach us, guide us, and give us the blessing of our entire selves. They are resources for us to expose and explore. The feelings that we have suppressed are desperate to be integrated into ourselves. They are only harmful when they are repressed."

EMBRACING OUR EMOTIONS

Embracing our emotions is the key to healing. And the gift of embracing our emotions and allowing them to be present, is two fold. First, the emotion dissipates and loses it chokehold, as we feel and honor its presence. And second, when we gain the insight and wisdom of that emotion, we are able to shift the energy of it, to fuel for positive change.

Think about an emotion you have felt over the past few days watching the news or engaging in a political conversation on social media.

Maybe you've felt anger, anxiety, frustration or fear.

Simply breathe into connection with that emotion and give it a voice. You can listen to the wisdom of your emotion and hear its wisdom, by asking yourself:

"What is the voice of this emotion trying to communicate or guide me to do?"

43

Maybe the voice your anger is screaming, "I can no longer sit back and watch the injustices that are occurring. I must be a part of the change, I desperately want to see."

Maybe the voice of your anxiety is saying to you, "Self care must be higher on your list in these challenging times. Make your well-being a priority today, with exercise, yoga, prayer, meditation, eating well, rest, focusing on gratitude, giving attention to the things that are going well in your life, or just unplugging from it all, for a period of time."

The voice of your frustration may be signaling, "It's ok to let other people disagree with you. Do the inner work to heal the places you are being triggered and you will be able to let it go."

By giving our emotions a voice, two things happen. First, we begin to connect more deeply with how we feel and by doing this, the emotion dissipates. Second, we gain the wisdom of our emotions. This very wisdom often directs us toward the action we need to take to move beyond the intensity of our emotional experience and begin to create change in the specific situation, we are experiencing.

Most importantly, once you have gained the insightful wisdom your emotion has given you, take action. Take an action that is aligned with what you want more of in your relationships, your community, your life and our country.

TRANSFORMING MY OUTRAGE

Last week, I was outraged by people attacking the press at a Trump rally. Here's how I processed through the outrage I was feeling and used it as fuel, for positive change.

First, I acknowledged it by simply breathing into this emotion. I identified the feeling located high in my chest.

Second, I gave it a voice by asking myself, "What is the voice of this emotion, trying to communicate or guide me to do?" As I listened to the wisdom, the voice of my outrage said, "Don't get weary. This is a dark time in our country and you must stay strong, centered and focused on expressing your truth and taking action that's aligned with what you want more of in your life and the world around you."

Third, I took action. I connected deeply with the importance of having a free press in our democracy, and made a commitment to myself to continue expressing my truth; to continue writing this book to share ways to process through the emotional upset, that can drain our energy and block us from feeling empowered enough to affect change.

YOUR WOUNDED SELF

So why is anger the predominant emotion in many of our political conversations right now?

Very simply, because anger is a healthy response when values are being violated. Take any issue and pick either side of the political aisle, and you can find a host of valid reasons to be angry. You can surely find an injustice currently taking place somewhere in our government, our country or the world that evokes anger within you.

The other reason anger is being awakened in a huge way, is that our wounded selves are being triggered and affected by the issues we are being faced with in this country.

Our wounded self is the part of us that holds onto repressed emotions, unresolved events and painful relationships from our past.

And like a scab being ripped off a physical wound, our wounded self can be re-affected when some-

thing in our current experience reminds us of something painful and unresolved from the past.

Like I shared in chapter one, my wounded self is
the part of me that is sensitive to others being bullied and must call it out, when I see it happening.

We will be exploring more about how to tend to
and heal your wounded self, in future chapters, so
you can use your unresolved emotions or trauma
from the past as an opportunity to heal, instead of
projecting your pain or hurt onto others.

Remember the ultimate measure of whether your
anger will be healing or destructive, invaluable or
wasteful, is in how you choose to use it. And the
only way to utilize the energy of your emotions for
positive change, is to first process through them.

The next time you feel anger manifest as tightness
in your chest, or anxiety show up as a pit in your
stomach, remind yourself to process through how
you are feeling before you respond or engage with
any one, in any way.

In the next chapter, we will dive into one of the
emotions that almost everyone in this country has
felt over the past two years. And that's, anxiety.

Want More? Listen as I guide you through the
exercise below on audio. Find the "Anger" audio at
www.dianealtomare.com/angeraudio

ANGER PROCESS

Get settled, take a few deep breaths and allow yourself to focus on reconnecting with the wisdom and
guidance of your anger.

1. First, close your eyes and turn all of your
   focus and awareness inside. As you take a
   deep breath, get present to focusing on just
   this moment, right here and right now. Let
   go of anything that would get in the way
   of you giving yourself this dedicated, unin-
   terrupted time.

2. Take another deep breath and as you drop
   into the space around your heart, find a
   connection to the anger present within
   you. Maybe you feel it as a tightness in
   your chest, a pit in your stomach or a lump
   in your throat. Maybe you feel it coursing
   through your veins. Maybe it's a feeling of
   being out of control or an inability to
   change what's happening. Just spend a few
   moments honoring your anger.

3. Imagine that as you connect with your
   anger, this emotion has a message for you.
   Take a deep breath and ask your anger,

"What are you trying to communicate to me?" "What is your message or wisdom for me?" "What injustice or violation of my values, am I seeing?"

4. Maybe your anger is here to help you take action, set a boundary, get involved, express your voice, have your truth be heard or communicate something important to someone specific.

5. Take another deep breath and a few moments to jot down some notes about the wisdom and message your anger has for you. Trust whatever you're feeling, sensing or writing, even if it doesn't make sense and even if it feels uncomfortable.

6. Finally, breathe into your heart and notice if you feel lighter, more peaceful, more energized or have more clarity after communicating with your anger.

7. Give yourself a few moments to sit in this place of peace, clarity and renewed energy, as you allow it to emanate through every cell of your body. Then open your eyes, as you bring this renewed energy with you into your day.

RELINQUISHING ANXIETY

Hatred and anger flooding social media, breaking news streaming moment by moment, Russian interference in our elections, new allegations in the Mueller investigation, Trump in opposition to his own administration, the never ending tweets and the list goes on and on.

There's so much division, a lot of chaos and much that is still hanging in the balance. All of this uncertainty in these uncertain times equates to many of us feeling anxiety.

Anxiety is a feeling that arises when we are being affected by something, we don't have control over. And frankly, there's so much we are witnessing on a daily basis in our country and government that most likely, won't be changing any time soon.

However, we have a lot more power than we often exert. And in these uncertain times, it is especially critical to connect with what we can do and how we can affect change. How we can speak out. Take action. Vote. Stop burying our head in the sand. Be courageous. Be active instead of passive. And ultimately, be a part of the change that must take place.

One of my friends shared:

I'm waking up with an "adrenaline rush" nearly every morning...NO alarm clock...just underlying anxiety about what TODAY may bring...I've never had this before.

I know from talking with many people about what's happening politically in this country that many of us are feeling some sense of anxiety on a daily basis. It's essential to acknowledge that this continual state of anxiety is toxic to our health.

Not only is it extremely physically damaging to our well-being, anxiety is detrimental to our daily lives because it often drives us to be reactive, instead of intentional.

Anxiety can be a strong influencer in the moment, because we often resort to grasping for anything that will make the uncomfortable, unsettling feeling go away. From this reactionary place, we often do what's easy or comfortable, instead of what's right. And most of the time our actions aren't aligned with what's in our highest and best interest, individually or collectively.

This is exactly what happens when people project their raw emotions onto others on social media. Just to release that emotion and in an effort to not feel the anxiety, anger or upset, we eject it from our body. We blurt out how we are feeling, without considering the repercussions or effect on ourselves or others.

This is also what Donald Trump does on Twitter, often. He projects his raw emotions of anxiety, fear, anger or upset onto the American people because he simply can't "be" with how he's feeling or process through his emotions, in a healthy way.

Here are a few examples of the president talking to the American people through his tweets:

"This is a terrible situation and Attorney General Jeff Sessions should stop this Rigged Witch Hunt right now, before it continues to stain our country any further. Bob Mueller is totally conflicted, and his 17 Angry Democrats that are doing his dirty work are a disgrace to USA!"

"The Failing New York Times wrote a story that made it seem like the White House Councel had TURNED on the President, when in fact it is just the opposite – & the two Fake reporters knew this. This is why the Fake News Media has become the Enemy of the People. So bad for America!"

"Lebron James was just interviewed by the dumbest man on television, Don Lemon. He made Lebron look smart, which isn't easy to do. I like Mike!"

This is certainly not the kind of leadership that many Americans are used to, or expect from the oval office. However despite this, many people claim they like this president's no-nonsense, 'tell it like it is' way of communicating.

Here are a couple of my friends that admire this quality:

"Proud to say he's my president! What I like about Trump is he doesn't sugar coat anything."

"I may not agree with the way Trump says things, but he has a big heart and I like that he tells it like it is. It's the liberals, who are angry and mean."

On the flip side, there are many people that don't like Trump's insults of others and find them egregious and unacceptable. James Clapper, Former Director of National Intelligence stated after Trump's aggressive comments and personal attacks at one of his rallies, "I just find this extremely disturbing. I really question his ability to be — his fitness to be — in this office and I also am beginning to wonder about his motivation for it."

I personally agree with James Clapper and don't see any benefit to the president of the United States insulting people, calling people names or sharing his raw emotions via twitter, on a continual basis. In fact, the president's tweets heighten the emotional instability and level of anxiety in our country. And regardless of whether you agree with his policies or not, his intense rhetoric both at rallies and on twitter, trigger emotional intensity, putting more hatred and upset into our collective conversations.

Even more damaging, as the leader of United States of America, Donald Trump is setting a horrible example for people to follow. In the social media thread below, you will see some people resort to name calling, jabs and insults, much like the president does. Some are blatant and others more insidious. Regardless, they are a reflection of the upset and anxiety many people feel and simply don't know what to do with.

SOCIAL MEDIA THREAD

Mary: Trump has accomplished so much already. Here are just a few things this administration has already done: Our economy is stronger, the unemployment rate has dropped to one of the lowest, our relationship with Israel is strong, he dismantled the horrible Iran nuclear deal, 3.2 trillion in tax cuts, denuclearization of North Korea, deployment of the National Guard to secure our borders, harmful reverse discrimination and the list goes on and on.

Carrie: Thanks Mary, I so agree with you! The list of accomplishments keeps growing. He is fulfilling his promises and more. He has done so much in so little time and people sit here and complain about a few negative words that come out of his mouth. Get over it! He's doing exactly what we elected him to do.

Morgan: Mary, much of that is good but the list of harmful things is even longer. Also, you can't list denuclearization – it hasn't happened. A factual statement would be "had a talk with Kim Jong Un about denuclearization."

Carrie: Morgan, tick tock...I'm still waiting on the list of harmful things. Put your money where your mouth is.

Morgan: Carrie, I honestly don't have the energy – but if you're truly interested, start with the environment, then go to education, then look at the G7, NATO, the UN, then look at taxpayer money spent on golf trips, take a look at the emoluments clause and so forth. It's an extensive and complicated list.

Knowing you're probably concerned with "fake news" be sure not to spread the denuclearization statement as it hasn't progressed past one conversation, and the US conceding things to NK, in the "hopes" of denuclearization.

Carrie: Morgan, finally. Thought you were bluffing.

Morgan: Carrie, I was being polite in responding to you, by pointing you in areas you could look up – if you were truly interested. You're obviously not, similarly you seem to have a hard time admitting that Trump kissed Kim Jong Un's ass and got nothing in return. Such a great deal maker.

Rebecca: Wow Carrie, so you refuse to do your own research to also learn about the incredibly harmful things that Trump and his administration have done since taking office, and then belittle Morgan for not wanting to do your research for you? I'll counterpoint every "good" point you listed: 1. Strong Economy: he inherited a strong economy from Obama, who got us out of the second potential Great Depression if you recall when he took office. Under Obama, Wall Street was the highest it's been since the 1930s. 2. Strong US/Israel relationship: do you even understand the Israeli/Palestinian "situation?" And do you agree that the U.S. should blindly 100% side with Israel, because I don't. Are you aware that what is Israel, was actually taken from the Palestinians after WW2 and given to Jewish/Israeli's so they would have a safe homeland. 3. "harmful reverse discrimination?" OMG! okay I see where you stand now and who you are. Do you have any friends of color, particularly any black friends – if so, then ask them about discrimination – every darn day of their lives. They do not have access to the same level of education, paying jobs, etc. as white people (which I'm assuming you are?) – and black people in particular, are most definitely discriminated against with regards to college entrances, jobs, etc. There are actual social science studies out there to prove this. 4. Denuclearization of N. Korea you are incorrect! They discussed it, but there are New satellite images that show North Korea has made rapid improvements to the infrastructure at its Yongbyon Nuclear Scientific Research Center – a facility used to produce weapons-grade fissile material, according to an analysis published by 38 North, a prominent North Korea monitoring group (so, this is not "fake news"). On other notes: Trump is the rudest, most divisive POTUS ever, calling people who disagree with him and call him out on his lies (which is every day, quite literally) and his horrible legislation. He's attacking our long-standing allies UK, Canada, Germany...you're okay with that? How do you feel about the fact that a dictatorship= Russia, meddled in our election and created quite literally fake news/fake social media accounts and stories, to throw the election to Trump? You're okay with that? Tell me how you feel about GOP Congressmen going to Russia last week to discuss getting rid of sanctions against Russia? He's putting in place tariffs that Canada and China are retaliating against and which economists say will increase the cost of a huge number of products we buy here in the U.S. (=inflation) and the tax cuts, are not going to help anyone long-term except for the very rich 1-5% so if that's you, then I see why you support him. He's a sexist misogynist who has cheated on all his wives. He just yesterday belittled the #metoo movement – literally making fun of men and women who are victims of sexual abuse. And the only way that Obama made America "divisive" is if someone were a racist and pissed off that a black man was POTUS.

Rebecca: Carrie, here's that research for you re: the 10 WORST things that Trump has done since taking office. I hope you are open to reading it.

Carrie: This is hilarious! Are you kidding? The stock market skyrocketed right after Trump was elected. Before him, the economy was stagnant. And just to set the record straight, I didn't belittle Morgan. Just seriously thought she was bluffing.

Carrie: Liberals are hilarious! I don't have to say much, and you all go hysterical. All a conservative has to do is disagree.

Mary: Liberals, go to your #safespace.

Diane Altomare: Carrie and Mary, we are not doing that here, in working to heal the emotional divide. Please re-read your last comments. It is not necessary to label, call people names or insult people to have a civil, kind conversation. Please do not comment here, if you are going to attack people.

Rebecca: Carrie you are quite literally not open to facts. The economy was most certainly not stagnant under 8 years of Obama. FACTS DURING OBAMA'S 8 YEARS: The economy gained a net 11.6 million jobs. The unemployment rate dropped to below the historical norm. Average weekly earnings for all workers were up 4% after inflation. After-tax corporate profits also set records, as did stock prices. The S&P 500 index rose 166%. The number of people lacking health insurance dropped by 15 million. Premiums rose, but more slowly than before. The federal debt owed to the public rose 128%. Deficits were rising as Obama departed. Home prices rose 20%. But the home ownership rate hit the lowest point in half a century. Illegal immigration declined: The Border Patrol caught 35% fewer people trying to get into the U.S. from Mexico. Wind and solar power increased 369%. Coal production declined 38%. Carbon emissions from burning fossil fuel dropped 11 percent. Production of handguns rose 192 percent, to a record level. The murder rate dropped to the lowest on record in 2014, then rose and finished at about the same rate as when Obama took office.

Morgan: Mary, why do you assume we are "triggered" or in need of a "safe space?" Is it because we are coming at you with facts?

Rebecca: Carrie and Mary, you are doing what

your POTUS does and instead of being able to log-ically discuss facts, you hurl insults or have noth-ing factual to counter with or discuss. #safespace and similar comments is akin to a childish bully kid on the playground who doesn't like a kid. Sad. Sorry, I have zero tolerance for people spouting lies and half-truths and putting it out there as fact. When you ask these women about Russia – crick-ets. When you provide them with facts on Obamas economy numbers – crickets. It's useless.

What's happening with many of these posts and this one specifically, is unresolved emotions and feelings of powerlessness are being projected all over the place. Because we can't change what's happening immediately and don't know what to do with how we're feeling, many in a state of desperation or frus-tration, haphazardly fling their emotional upset into the conversation and onto each other.

HEALING THE DIVISION

However, despite the difficulty many people have, conversing in a kind, civil manner, we still need to talk to each other. And regardless of how messy and difficult it can be to talk with people who disagree with us politically, it's imperative we continue to have conversations with each other, to bridge the gap and heal this division. As you witnessed in the social media thread above, the jabs, insults and attacks are what threaten this reconnection many of us are seeking and instead, create more animosity and upset.

When we attack or criticize somebody else's point of view and don't give them the grace of honoring how they feel, not only do we create more hatred and chaos, we miss the whole point of the emotional awakening this is intended to be. Fighting against each other will continue to divide us. Choosing to courageously look within and process through our emotional upset is what will not only heal us individually, but will heal this divide.

The choice is ours to make, often on a moment to moment basis. It is not always easy to do because so many of us are emotionally charged by what's happening. But it is the work, we must each do right now. The emotional well-being of our country and our democracy depends on it.

TWO OPPOSING SIDES IN HARMONY

Right about now, you may be thinking to yourself,

"Is processing through my emotions and embracing my shadows really going to change this deep emotional divide and bring more harmony into our political conversations and our country?" It's a great question to ask, given the insurmountable evidence that the emotional landscape seems to be getting more heated and the division seems to be widening. So here's a bit of hope to sprinkle into your consciousness, to inspire you to keep going and know that not only is this possible, but it's happening when people do the work to process through their emotional upset and express how they feel, in a healthy way.

Here's a story of inspiration and a true example of two opposing political sides living in harmony. A dear friend shared her relationship breakthrough with me:

"I've started dating an old boyfriend from 30 years ago who is a Republican, thinks like a Republican and didn't vote because he hated both candidates. He came along right at the time I started digging in with your work. He's my test. We were able to have a one hour conversation the other night about politics and Roe V. Wade. He pushes back on me, his political perspective combined with his Christian faith.

*We disagreed on a few big things. I could feel myself
start to boil then I just came back to the trigger point.
I made it through and we came out on the other side
without harm or foul.*

*I'm convinced that this work is working for me.
Thank you!"*

You can imagine how ecstatic I was to receive this
news after all the hostility, name calling and insults
I've witnessed in many of the posts I've shared with
you thus far. As I shared her story, I replied, "This
is absolutely amazing! And brings a huge smile to
my face. This is truly what healing the emotional
divide is all about. You are so inspiring! Thank you
for sharing this, as many people are losing hope."
And I added, "I am hoping this will inspire others, to
know that it's possible for all of us to find this place
of connection with people in our lives that disagree
with us politically. It's not always easy; it doesn't
mean emotions don't arise, but it can absolutely be
our reality, if we are willing to process through our
own emotional upset and listen to and honor each
other's point of view."

COMBAT DAILY ANXIETY

So given the anxiety, powerlessness and fear that many of us are feeling as well as the divisive, fragile state of our country and the inability to stop the daily barrage of breaking news that's occurring, let's dive into what you can do to counter the impact all this may be having on you and your relationships. By acknowledging and processing through the anxiety you are feeling, you will not only be able to honor your emotional upset but can have compassion for others when they are emotionally charged, as well.

First, it's essential to identify the root cause of your anxiety. By understanding what and why something specifically makes you feel panic or uncertainty, you will be better equipped to know what to do in the moments you feel the anxiety arising. Let's explore two of the most common roots of anxiety: powerlessness and fear.

Powerlessness is defined as a lack of ability, influence or power. I can personally attest to feeling this on a sometimes daily basis, as a result of what's taking place with this administration and in our country. Simply watching the news, seeing one atrocity after the other flash before my eyes and thinking, "It's hopeless. There's nothing I can do to change this." One of my friends shared a similar sentiment:

*"I feel paralyzed over what we all witnessed yester-
day, watching Trump side with Putin, standing in
opposition to our Intelligence Community and the
United States. Now we know that Cult 45 is a treasonous traitor. I do not know what to do with this anxiety, other than meditate. Maybe I'll just drink a lot
of wine and numb it all out for a few days."*

Feeling paralyzed is the direct result of the belief
that you are powerless. Here's a quick, simple way
to relinquish this anxiety and regain connection to
what may better serve you and your intention for
your day.

First, when this emotion arises, simply identify its
opposite. The opposite of powerlessness is empowered or the feeling of being in control.

Your next step is to focus on something, within
your control. Take action somewhere in your life,
where you can affect change.

Here are a few questions to ask yourself, to inspire
action:

- *What can I do today to take action on something that's important to me?*
- *What action is aligned with the values I cherish?*

Many people I have connected with, have shared feeling powerless about some of the policies implemented by this administration. Here's how Beth, one of my clients, transformed her feelings of powerlessness into inspired action.

Diane, as soon as the San Diego detainment facility allows healthcare professional volunteers to enter, I plan on volunteering my time to soothe these poor motherless babies and toddlers.

I've learned through this immigration crisis and from doing your development work, that my compulsion to engage in social media, including the rage that builds up inside, are emotional triggers that are pushed when I don't feel safe. I was raised in a mentally and physically abusive home by a rage-aholic mother. My buttons are always about feeling unsafe or feeling unlovable.

When people justify the horrific human rights violations against these poor innocent children and their parents who are running for their lives to a "safe place", it makes me afraid that we are creating another Nazi Germany situation with bigotry, hatred, intolerance and internment camps for people

*our government doesn't like. My fear buttons are trig-
gering my angry, combative buttons.*

*Doing the work is really hard, but this is what
HAS to happen if we have any hope for bringing this
country together so we can heal and make a better
life for our kids and the 2,300 orphans we've just created.*

*Thank you for your tireless dedication to the
process.*

By connecting with her feelings of rage, she was able
to turn her emotional upset into a plan of action.

First, Beth acknowledged how she was feeling by
simply breathing into the upset and outrage that was
present. She identified the feeling as a nauseousness
in her stomach. Being a mother herself, she felt so
much pain for the parents that didn't know where
their children were or whether they were being cared
for.

Second, she gave the rage a voice by asking herself, "What is the voice of this emotion trying to
communicate or guide me to do?" As she listened,
the voice of her rage said, "You are fortunate and
have a responsibility to help these parents and children. Get involved. Speak out about this atrocity.

Volunteer at one of the facilities where these kids are housed."

Third, she created a plan of action.

The result of doing this emotional work was an immediate sense of relief, knowing she had a plan in place to be a part of the change. And although she couldn't reverse what had happened to these kids, she could have an impact on some of them by genuinely and lovingly caring for these children, when the time came.

Outrage is one of the emotions that's contributing to a feeling of constant anxiety for many of us. Another one, is fear.

Remember the tweets about Rocket Man, Trump's name for North Korean Leader Kim Jong Un? Here is one of the many, Trump has tweeted:

North Korean Leader Kim Jong Un just stated that the "Nuclear Button is on his desk at all times." Will someone from his depleted and food starved regime please inform him that I too have a Nuclear Button, but it is a much bigger & more powerful one than his, and my Button works!

Kim Jong Un of North Korea, who is obviously a madman who doesn't mind starving or killing his people, will be tested like never before!

My anxiety during the times of these dangerous tweets was deeply rooted in fear; the fear that nuclear war was going to break out.

And as if that's not enough to fear, another huge area of concern for many people is the ratcheting up of Trump's dangerous rhetoric towards the media. Here are a few of the mirage of tweets, where the president is attacking our free press:

"The Fake News hates me saying that they are the Enemy of the People only because they know it's TRUE. I am providing a great service by explaining this to the American People. They purposely cause great division & distrust. They can also cause War! They are very dangerous & sick!"

"The Fake News is working overtime. Just reported that, despite the tremendous success we are having with the economy & all things else, 91% of the Network News about me is negative (Fake). Why do we work so hard in working with the media when it is corrupt? Take away credentials?"

"Too bad a large portion of the Media refuses to

*report the lies and corruption having to do with the
Rigged Witch Hunt – but that is why we call
them FAKE NEWS!"*

*"THE FAKE NEWS MEDIA IS THE OPPOSI-
TION PARTY. It is very bad for our Great Country....BUT WE ARE WINNING!"*

In one year alone, the president referred to our
media, as the"fake news"320 times.

With this emotional intensity continually poured
into our consciousness, we have to remain diligent
in alleviating these high levels of anxiety and fear.
Although it can be tough to continually process
through this extreme emotional upset on a daily
basis, it's even more impossible to ignore. It's vitally
essential to take the time to sift through our emotions, express them in a healthy way and do what's
necessary to emerge stronger, so we are able to face
whatever is yet to come.

First, when this emotion arises, simply identify its
opposite. The opposite of fear is a feeling of being
calm or confident.

Your next step is to do something that brings you
the feeling of being calm. Or take action somewhere

in your life, where you normally feel a sense of confidence, so you can reconnect to these feelings. Here are a few questions, to ask yourself:

- *What reconnects me to the confidence and peace within me?*
- *What calms me or makes me feel centered?*

Then pick one of these, to help you regain your center or evoke calm feelings:

- *Prayer*
- *Exercise*
- *Yoga*
- *Meditation*
- *Deep breathing*
- *Reading uplifting books*
- *Focusing on what you are grateful for*
- *Being around positive people*
- *Processing through emotional upset*
- *Unplugging for a period of time*

By acknowledging what you need to do to feel more calm and confident and then taking the corresponding actions, you will reconnect with and re-awaken the emotional experience, you want more of.

Here's how one of my clients transformed his fear into inspired action and hope.

Kent was angry and at the same time, felt panic and anxiety about the future of our country.

First, he acknowledged how he was feeling by simply breathing into the anxiety and anger that was present. He identified the feeling as a clenching in his fists and a tightness in his chest.

Second, he gave the anger a voice by asking himself, "What is the voice of this emotion trying to communicate or guide me to do?" As he listened, the voice of his anger said, "Take your passion for our country and do something. Gather everyone you can to vote and be a part of the change."

Third, he took action. Every time he had the opportunity to express his passion, he implored people to vote. He also committed to gathering everyone he could on Election Day and encouraged each one of them to go to the ballot box and have their voice heard.

By taking action and using the energy of his passion as fuel for change, Kent felt empowered and hopeful, instead of hopeless and powerless, like he previously had. Whenever the anxiety or anger arose, he used it as inspiration to speak out more and take action.

Another one of my friends shared how she has been turning her anxiety into action, as well:

> *"So far, for me, I've taken action by participating in marches and rallies in support of these issues. I've also made donations to various groups and have spoken up at my council meetings. I signed up for notifications on issues that are important to me and submit comments on calls to action, to my representatives. These things haven't been easy, sometimes they're exhausting, but I press on. I've always been one to volunteer in my community, but I think I'll refocus to organizations that really need it. The one good thing coming out of this administration is that it is bringing a lot of issues to light that we may have ignored in our previous comfort. Stay woke my friends, stay woke!"*

As we gain insight into why we are feeling anger, anxiety or sadness, we understand more specifically what we need to do in the moments these emotions arise, both to diminish the intensity and create more of what we desire.

Make no mistake, this is an intense, dark time in our country's history. Even if you aren't paying attention to the daily happenings or minute by minute coverage, most of us are being affected by the dark, destructive energy that's present in our country right now. It's essential to be aware of how this may be affecting you, so you can combat this negative energy by taking immaculate care of yourself physically, mentally and emotionally. And as we've been talking about, use the energy of your emotions for positive change.

A couple of my friends shared how it's impacting them:

"As an empath, this negative energy that you speak of is very, very real. I hope your readers actually really understand the power that Trump has over this nation. He is inciting fear, anger and hatred. As someone who works with energy and vibration there's a lot of black black black stuff out there. Protecting our energy is really important."

"I let myself feel the range of emotions. I feel shock, I feel anger, I feel fear. Then I take a deep breath & remind myself of the hundreds & thousands of good people who are examples of fairness, goodness

& TRUTH in our nation. May we not run, hide, or let this president win through his fear tactics! For me, the president's rallies confirm that there is much work to be done. I come ALIVE and ask myself 'What is one thing I can do today to bring forth change?' We each are here at this time for a reason! Let's challenge what is & imagine what can be: A more peaceful nation/planet for us all."

The Antidote To Anxiety

Stepping into action is one of the most powerful ways to alleviate anxiety and literally stop it, in its tracks.

Think about a recent time you felt immense anxiety. Maybe it was just earlier today, as you saw breaking news flash across your phone. As you contemplated what you were reading, you may have felt a pit in your stomach or a feeling of powerlessness wash over you. Maybe you thought, "OMG. Here we go again. And there's nothing I can do about it." So you just pressed on with your day, passed over what you just saw and pretended that you didn't feel disgust, outrage or panic.

Let's take a look at all that transpired in that one

moment you read that tweet or skimmed through the article on your phone.

In the very moment you received that alert of breaking news, first your brain attempted to make sense of what you were reading. You then had an emotional reaction to that piece of information and most likely also realized, you had no control over what was happening. Then you made a split minute decision, regardless of your feelings of upset, sadness or anger to continue on with your day because you have a job to do, children to raise and a home to take care of.

This is one of the insidious ways our energy is being drained on a daily basis and what's contributing to many people feeling an overwhelming sense of anxiety.

The other thing that's contributing to this high level of anxiety is the amount of chaos and atrocities, we both see and hear about on a daily basis. It can simply be too much to process through, especially if we are not consciously aware of or making a point to pay attention to how we're feeling, as a result of what we are watching, reading or hearing.

Although you may have continued on with your day after hearing about that specific atrocity, many of those unresolved feelings that arose from reading that breaking news, are now simmering within you. On top of it, to add even more to the anxiety or emotional exhaustion, when we feel like there's nothing we can do about it, we have to find some way to cope with what's occurring. Many people, encumbered with more anxiety than they can process, are eating more, drinking more alcohol, taking antidepressants or in a state of continual outrage, panic or adrenal fatigue. Some people have shared that they are more irritable. While others, have chosen to check out and not pay attention, or engage.

In order to be a part of the change in these challenging times, we must continually strive to find a balance between being in acceptance of what's happening and at the same time feeling empowered to take action, that ultimately affects the change we want to see.

So what can you do to be a part of the solution? As one of my friends shared, she asks herself this question every day: *"What is one thing I can do today to bring forth change?"* This is a great question to ask and a great reminder to put in your daily calendar.

Sometimes, the answer to this question may be as simple as you bringing more love and compassion to yourself and those around you. Or as big, as choosing to run for office.

In the next chapter, we will explore specific ways to transform one of the most immobilizing emotions into inspired action. And that's, fear.

4

TRANSCENDING FEAR

Fear can paralyze and immobilize; it's an emotion that holds immense power to simply shut you down or render you powerless.

Bob Woodward and Robert Costa, reporters of The Washington Post, interviewed Donald Trump in March of 2016, before he was president. Trump said to them, "Real power is ... I don't even want to use the word: fear."

President Richard Nixon echoed Trump's sentiments about fear and leadership when he said, "People react to fear, not love. They don't teach that in Sunday school, but it's true."

I asked my friends on social media what they most fear right now about the way this administration is leading, as well as the division in our country.

Here's what a few said:

"I see the harshness of racism becoming more and more acceptable by people calling police of black people swimming, sitting in Starbucks, moving into Air BNB; women on golf courses for "playing too slow." This is what happens when the president calls Mexicans murderers and refers to black people from "Shit Hole Countries."

"I find the deregulation of water, air, food and banking pollutants is something that affects me greatly."

"Trump tearing up trade deals with Iran, Paris Climate Change, TPP, NAFTA, all will make life more difficult."

"His childish name calling of people he is jealous of or just hates because they are in another party, manifests itself in dehumanizing people who don't agree with him, as opposed to simply debating issues."

"I do not feel my life is better. The trade wars with

allies, the Russian interference in the election that he will never acknowledge. There's so much."

Fear, much like anger is a common emotion in turbulent times. Read any social media conversation with people of differing political views and you will see fear being projected all over the place.

What will differ from person to person and comment to comment is the actual thing or experience, each individual fears the most. That is often the point of contention in many of these political debates.

The one thing we can often agree on, however; the one fear that tows party lines is the fear of losing something each of us holds dear.

As you can see in this social media interaction, the loss of our collective ability to civilly connect and communicate with each other is what drives the passion for my work to heal the emotional divide in this country.

Although many people have criticized the way I'm choosing to do this emotional healing work, using the energy of my emotions as a catalyst, is the impetus for all that I'm doing, including the writing of this book.

SOCIAL MEDIA THREAD

Mark: It appears the "powers that be" have accomplished their mission. Diane, I don't know you, but you are a healer. We are in the midst of the sixth extinction and it will be those that transcend, that will survive and help others survive. You are smarter than this to buy into the divisiveness. It's hard not to, I fight it every day. But neither you nor I, nor most Americans, actually know what the real truth is. We see only what is fed to us with a specific purpose.

It is your duty as a healer to look at things objectively and from a place of peace. Men like Trump or Obama, and women like Hillary are straw men (straw people, jeez) to distract us and emotionally charge us. Look deeper. It's not kids at the border... that is puffed up click bait. Next month it will be some other bullshit. You're alienating half of your audience for the sake of righteous indignation. That's wasted energy.

C'mon....transcend! Overcoming fabricated divisive hate would be a great topic for your next book. Healing the rift. This country needs it. Just give me a second page dedication.

Diane Altomare: Let's stop focusing on whether I'm doing this right or wrong Mark. I have had the benefit of watching this unfold over the past few months, and it is important that we are each able to have our views, without being attacked, which includes me. I do not need to be neutral, in order to teach and guide people on how to deal with their emotional projections; to not attack others that have different views. If we can stop focusing on whether I'm doing this right or wrong, and each individually dive into our own emotions, that is the work of healing the emotional divide. I understand that you and many others disagree with the way I am doing things, but it is working, when people are willing to look inside and deal with how they are being affected and triggered. Stop focusing on me and my views, close your eyes and deal with your own emotional upset. That is the work of healing the emotional divide. Your outrage at me, is exactly the reason, that I need to be able to share my views. We have to each, get better at allowing each other to feel how we feel, without attacking, demeaning, belittling or making each other wrong. I respect your views, and how you feel...But continually focusing on me, isn't the focus of the work we're doing on this page.

Mark: I understand. This would make a great show topic. Deana would be a great contact for you. She has a show taping now, it's a very passionate show and you would make a great guest.

Mark is not the only one that has criticized me for sharing my political views and not the only one that feels I would be of better service, if I was politically inexpressive or neutral.

However, there is a reason I'm not neutral and why I have chosen to be clear and express wholeheartedly how I feel on different political issues. First, I can't lead or teach something I am not doing myself. And it would be hypocritical to ask others to share their political views and lovingly agree to disagree with people who oppose how they feel, if I as a woman in the United States of America, stood here inexpressive, teaching something that I myself wasn't experiencing, didn't have the courage to do or wasn't an example of. My intention in helping to heal the emotional divide is that we can each get better at expressing how we feel, without attacking, belittling, labeling or calling each other names. My mission is that simple and although sharing my views may complicate that, it truly is the only way to do this authentically and with lasting impact.

In this chapter, we are going to explore exactly how you can transform the energy of your fear into fuel for positive change. How you can transcend this immobilizing emotion and use it as motivation to create more of what you want to see in the world, instead of allowing it to render you powerless.

COURAGE

The most powerful antidote to fear is courage. However, courage can seem like a world away when you are in the grips of something that terrifies you; something you are deathly afraid of. So how do you make this leap? By connecting deeply with your truth, who you are and what you are here to accomplish at this time in your life.

Embracing and exuding passion for any issue you value, for your freedom of speech, for our democracy, for women's rights, for minority rights or for human decency has the power to arm you with the exact energy and courage you need to transcend your fear and step into extraordinary action.

Remember how many Americans were outraged and spoke up about this administration's zero tolerance policy? Americans spoke so vehemently, that the president and the administration reversed their atrocious decision to implement a policy that separated children from their parents at our border. That's what passion for an issue looks like and how it manifests itself into courageous action and extraordinary results.

As one of my friends shared, "What do you stand for?"

By getting deeply connected to what you stand for and what you value as well as what you fear losing, you can access the very truth, passion and courage that will catapult you into action. The energy of your fear can be the very impetus that drives you to stand for what you most value.

Let's look at how this works.

TRANSFORMING FEAR

Throughout the Trump presidency, I have been outraged by Trump's attacks on the media. Our freedom of expression, and the media holding our leaders accountable and protecting our democracy is something that I hold, in the highest regard. My fear of losing these freedoms is high on the list of issues that cause me great anxiety.

Here's how I transcended my fear and used it as fuel to inspire action.

First, I acknowledged the fear was present, by simply breathing into the emotion. I identified this fear located in the pit of my stomach.

Second, I gave it a voice by asking myself, "What is the voice of this emotion trying to communicate or guide me to do?" As I listened to the wisdom, the voice of my fear said, "Freedom of speech is one of the things you hold most dear. Even as a little girl, you were talkative and self-expressive. Imagine living in a country where you didn't have the freedom to say how you feel or the freedom to stand up for what you believe is right. As a woman in the United States of America, it's unfathomable. And you must stand up for this deep core belief and fight for freedom of speech and this country's democracy."

Third, I took action. I have made it my mission to understand the inner workings of what may be happening in our country. I have read, studied and analyzed what's truly going on; why the president is viciously attacking our media and indirectly, our freedom of speech. And then I chose to speak out about the danger of our president attacking our free press, on my weekly radio show. I also began connecting with journalists to share my appreciation and gratitude for their professionalism; for the essential work they do every day, to protect our democracy and our country.

Now, it's your turn to transcend what you most fear and turn it into fuel, to inspire action.

First, close your eyes and take a moment to get still. Then acknowledge your fear by simply breathing into connection with it.

Second, identify where you feel this fear in your body. Is it an overall nauseous feeling, or showing up as panic in your solar plexus or a pit in your stomach?

Spend a few moments connecting with what your life would be like, without this freedom or experience.

Next, give it a voice. You can hear or sense the wisdom of your fear, by asking yourself:

"What is the voice of this emotion trying to communicate or guide me to do?"

Maybe the voice your fear is saying, "I can no longer sit back and watch these things I hold so dear being threatened. I must be a part of the change, I desperately want to see."

Or maybe you hear the voice of your fear signaling, "I won't be able to forgive myself if I stand by and watch the loss of women's rights, that generations of women have fought for. I have to do everything I can to ensure these rights are upheld."

Remember, by giving your fear a voice, two things happen. First, you connect more deeply with how you feel and by doing this, the emotion dissipates. Second, you gain the wisdom of your fear and this very insight directs you toward actions that will help you transcend this fear and create change.

Finally, once you have gained the insightful wisdom your fear has communicated, take action that's aligned with what you want more of in your life, your relationships, your community, and our country.

EXPRESSING YOUR TRUTH

One of the other fears, I have heard voiced time and time again throughout my work to heal the emotional divide, is how frightening it is for many people to share their true political views. They fear being insulted, attacked, labeled or ostracized like they've seen many others experience.

Many people are living a quiet desperation because they can't simply express, how they truly feel about what's happening. They fear repercussion from their spouse, family members, co-workers or company.

Here are just a few of my friends who have shared their fear of expressing how they feel politically:

"In a country where free speech is allowed, it's scary to even voice your opinion. I have close friends that I don't dare say what my political stance is, because anger and hatred is so rampant."

"My husband voted for Trump and my daughter, who is adopted, sobbed the day after the election when I had to tell her he won. She was afraid she would be deported. I reassured her, and then she asked about all her friends who work their asses off in the fields, what would happen to them and their children? This from my 12 year old! We are not able to discuss anything political in our home, and it almost split our marriage. I have such an emotional reaction whenever I hear someone support Trump. But I am trying to ask questions, to see where they are coming from."

"I get really angry when people, mostly my friends and colleagues, don't really respect the things that mean a lot to me personally. I feel like I can't say any-

thing, because I don't feel like my opinion is listened to or ever respected."

One of the reasons people fear sharing their views, is because of the rampant hostility many people bring into political conversations. And it certainly doesn't help to have the leader of our country emulating the behavior of a playground bully, as he often does, by getting defensive or lashing out at others when he's criticized or called out.

In this tweet, one of many, where Trump is on the defensive, he attacks the Special Council investigation led by Robert Mueller. Trump tweeted:

"Our relationship with Russia has NEVER been worse thanks to many years of U.S. foolishness and stupidity and now, the Rigged Witch Hunt!"

As you can see from this social media thread to follow, the insults and hostility emulate the President's destructive, condescending nature and tone.

SOCIAL MEDIA THREAD

Joe: Trump's obviously saying "way to go," idiot Obama and Liberals. Let's try to not twist things, Diane.

George: Joe, how can Diane twist facts? Give evidence.

Joe: Facts? I'm going off what Obama did to this country for eight straight years. Unfortunately, liberals are either blind or just don't want to accept it.

George: Joe, give me some of what you observed. Who knows, maybe you can convince me!

Joe: Nah, I don't feel like wasting my time with a smart ass. Who obviously is a huge liberal by looking at your profile. You just keep crying.

Samantha: Wow...such hateful and fearful talk. This is the divide Putin wants and is getting. Study history...we are so repeating it. No open mind to truly learn and listen to another point of view and when facts are asked, none are given because that would possibly show a wrinkle in the fabric of our belief. Do we even get our privileges? Instead, it's much easier to call out names and spit venom without truly learning and looking for the reality that is not backed by those with an agenda. How easy it is to be sold off. Like the frog put in cold water and slowly the temperature rises and the frog ends up getting cooked because the frog doesn't realize and feel the truth.

Sometimes, like in the post above, conversations get heated because people are arguing about whose facts are true. There really is no need to argue facts. Each one of us gets to trust our own intellect, what we see, how we feel and what is important to us. Our conversations must lean more towards listening and honoring each other's differing point of view, instead of arguing who's right or who's wrong.

When we argue, and try to prove we are right and the other person is wrong, we have already lost the battle. The only way to truly heal this emotional divide is to respect that we each have a different point of view and simply listen to what that is. This is how severed relationships will begin to mend and how our differences will be revered as something we value, instead of something that threatens to permanently split us apart.

Here's another example of the hostility present in many conversations. This time it was directed at me and the work I'm doing.

SOCIAL MEDIA THREAD

Candy: You keep saying you want to invite dialogue and heal the emotional divide, blah, blah, blah. It appears more as though it's quite self-serving, instead of helping anybody heal anything.

Diane Altomare: I lovingly disagree with you.

Why do you feel the need to attack me or what I'm doing Candy? We are doing powerful work here, in healing the emotional divide. And if it doesn't speak to you, I completely respect that.

Candy: It's clearly self-serving. Just don't see how this helps anything.

Diane Altomare: Dealing with our emotional upset and how we are projecting your anger, fear or anxiety onto other people, that we politically disagree with, takes courage to face, and it is not for everybody. If it doesn't speak to you, that's OK. We are doing awesome work here and I welcome calm, loving, civil conversation with you, Candy.

Margaret: Diane Altomare, I'm really starting to see what you're saying.

The difference in interactions, when people are reacting from a perceived insult (in this case, anything negative about the administration and the poor job they're doing), versus when people are genuinely sharing and furthering the conversation.

Evelyn: Blah, blah, blah? That's very dismissive language.

Candy: Evelyn, wasn't trying to be dismissive. Just a way to say "on and on."

Evelyn: Ok Candy...Thanks for clearing that up. Appreciate it.

Diane Altomare: Yes, Margaret! People often get stuck in their emotional upset, when I call the president out for what I view as disgraceful behavior, even though it has nothing to do with them. Here's the work in the moment anyone of us is triggered by what anyone else says: If you make it mean something about you, in that moment you have inner work to do to heal that projection. Healing the emotional divide happens when each one of us takes responsibility for our own emotional upset, and actually does the work to process through our emotions in a healthy way. The way to have conversations with people that disagree with you politically, in a kind loving compassionate way, is by processing through your emotions and healing yourself individually first. Some are willing to embrace this, and others just want to be angry and upset and project that onto other people. It truly is a choice we have to each make.

As you've witnessed in many of these conversations, when fear or upset is projected onto someone else, it creates division and animosity. However in this conversation, you can see the moment when the tides turn, when honoring another's viewpoint happens and understanding begins to take place.

Social Media Thread

Tammy: Proud to say Trump's my president! I wasn't a fan of Obama, but he was my president too. So to those who say not my president...when are you leaving?

Kim: Tammy, he may be this country's President but he is not one that I support or connect with on an ideological or emotional level. I have a right to that without being told to leave a country that I was born in 75 years ago.

Tammy: I agree you don't have to support him. That is your right. It just annoys me, when people say #notmypresident. He is your president, if you are an American. And so you know, I was not saying leave, in a hateful way. It just feels wrong, when people say that.

Kim: To explain why some people might say that he is "not their president" might be because they do no want to feel connected in any way to a person who has expressed himself in ways that they feel deeply offended by; regarding women, people from various ethnicities, the disabled, etc. If I were overseas, I would make it clear that as an American, I in no way support this.

Conversations like this, where we seek to understand each other's view even if we don't agree, can begin to bridge the gap and heal the division.

OUR DEMOCRACY HANGS IN THE BALANCE

The writing on the wall is stark and bold:

We must wake up and come together.

Most of us can feel this truth in our hearts. We may know this truth, as an urging from our anxiety to transcend the arguing in our conversations. Or may have heard this guidance from our fear, commanding us to stop contributing to the hatred or the division.

It is our responsibility, both individually and collectively to overcome our differences and rise above the darkness, that's present in our country. The more we are willing to process through our unresolved emotions and embrace our shadows, the more light we can bring to everyone and everything we touch.

A powerful question to ask yourself every day:

"Am I using this situation, experience or relationship to

*heal, emerge stronger and more whole, or am I stuck in
the emotional intensity of it?"*

If you are stuck in the intensity of your emotions,
simply connect with your emotion, give it a voice,
and then take the action your wisdom guides you to
take.

Our emotional upset is valid. Many of us are outraged, disgusted and scared. However, instead of
taking the intensity of our upset to our relationships
or social media, our work is to stop projecting our
upset, anger or fear onto each other and process
through our emotions so we can use the fuel of these
emotions to align with our values and affect change.
Our democracy and what we stand for as Americans
requires that we do this now, more than ever.

In the next chapter, we will dive into ways to overcome feelings of powerlessness, as you powerfully
step into action that empowers change.

OVERCOMING POWERLESSNESS

One of my dear friends, shared:

"I was just leaving a meeting and the alarm went off in the building. On the loudspeaker a voice said there was an emergency and we all had to leave. I fought back tears until I got in my car and then sat and balled my eyes out. What the 'bleep" is going on in this world? We hear of tragedy after tragedy, and you don't realize it's affecting you until moments like this."

Many of us can relate. We are on edge. Moments like this not only exemplify the inner anxiety we may be managing on a daily basis, but remind us of how powerless we are, at times.

Bloomberg weighed in on the anxiety and powerlessness two-thirds of Americans felt in November of 2017, just nine months after Donald Trump took the oath of office, as President of the United States:

"For those lying awake at night worried about health care, the economy, and an overall feeling of divide between you and your neighbors, there's at least one source of comfort: Your neighbors might very well be lying awake, too.

Almost two-thirds of Americans, or 63 percent, report being stressed about the future of the nation, and the "current social divisiveness" in America was reported by 59 percent of those surveyed as a cause of their own malaise."

Not only do many of us feel powerless, but we're exhausted by the lack of control we have over what's happening on a daily basis. And worse, the more exhausted we feel, the easier it is to throw our hands up in the air and simply resign to all this chaos, becoming our new normal. Many have simply checked out and turned away from it all.

As an Integrative Coach that has led thousands of people to embrace their shadows and make peace with their past, I have both studied and witnessed the psychological behavior of people for decades. I have become fascinated by the inner workings of what's happening in our society, as a result of this new level of intense emotional upset thrust into our daily lives by this administration, the media's coverage of it and the social media debates about it.

Part of what has contributed to Americans feeling powerless is we are being led by a president that has built his reputation on being a renegade and breaking just about every norm, we've grown accustomed to.

I along with millions of people have watched this president exemplify and lead our country with some of the worst human tendencies there are.

Dr. Deepak Chopra, a world-renowned pioneer in personal transformation says:

> "Trump has stripped away the facade, intoxicated by the "fun" of letting his demons run and discovering to his surprise (much as Nixon did) that millions of people roared with approval. In reality, Trump isn't bizarre or anomalous. He stands for something universal, something right before our eyes. It's an aspect of the human psyche that we feel embarrassed and ashamed of, which makes it our collective secret.
>
> Going back a century in the field of depth psychology, the secret side of human nature acquired a

special name: the shadow. The shadow compounds all the dark impulses—hatred, aggression, sadism, selfishness, jealousy, resentment, sexual transgression—that are hidden out of sight. When Trump indulges in rampant bad behavior and at the same time says to his riotous audiences, 'This is fun, isn't it?' he's expressing in public our ashamed impulse to stop obeying the rules."

One of the shadow impulses Trump runs wild with, is that of a street fighter: it's me, against anyone who disagrees with me. In Trump's world and unfortunately now in America, there are two worlds: one for Trump and the other, against Trump.

In this social media thread, you can clearly see those that are for Trump, and those who are against, either Trump's policies or more specifically, his behavior. The division is crystal clear. And this very lack of unity and the spirit with which people are fighting against each other, is part of what contributes to a feeling of powerlessness and the deep societal angst that's present.

MY POST

Please explain to me, Sarah Sanders, how you can represent and defend a president that attacks our media on a continual basis and also at the same time say, "A violent attack on innocent journalists doing their job is an attack on every American?"

What am I missing here?

Sarah Sander's tweet: "Strongly condemn the evil act of senseless violence in Annapolis, MD. A violent attack on innocent journalists doing their job is an attack on every American. Our prayers are with the victims and their families and friends."

And let me be clear, so people don't mince my words. I did not blame Trump...I didn't make that statement at all. However, Trump consistently does what Sarah Sanders is standing up against, when she says, "A violent attack on innocent journalists doing their job is an attack on every American."

And I agree with her statement. What is unacceptable, is that our president attacks the media and innocent journalists, almost daily.

SOCIAL MEDIA THREAD

Paul: Diane Altomare, how would you suggest our president address the fact that most news outlets have negative reports about him 90+% of the time? Where's the objectivity in that? While journalists personally may have disagreements about his policies, and well over 50% of them do (which is a whole other problem), they are supposed to be trained to give the facts and allow the readers to make their own conclusions. How old-fashioned and quaint that appears today. Journalism is almost wholly dead and advocacy agencies and propagandists is a better description of their current function. I'm glad that Pres. Trump is calling them out on it as they are little more than purveyors of "fake news" and "very fake news," especially when it comes to him and his agenda.

　Beth: 90% (and that's being kind) of what he gives journalists to report on is negative. Here's a funny thing, if you don't blatantly make a fool of yourself, disrespect your country, your predecessors, your colleagues, your citizens and your allies every day...the negative press would go *poof*.

　Paul: Beth, you may be too young to remember how Barry Goldwater was treated in 1964. His sanity and fitness for office were questioned by some hundred or more psychiatrists. Pres. Reagan got the same treatment as did Pres. Bush 43. All non-democrat officeholders are "dumb" "unenlightened" or "out-of-step with reality" when described by liberals. The fact that you don't see the pattern and similarity of the attacks doesn't make them untrue.

Beth: Paul, the fact that you're comparing Trump to Bush, Reagan, or any of our other beloved Presidents, regardless of party, shows how deep you've sunk into the MAGA hole.

Paul: Beth, attempting to communicate with you is to go through the looking glass for sure. Are you done with this pointless belittling or do you wish to do more of it?

Mike: Trump brings on the negative coverage because he does negative things. Read and watch the news then do a little research. If Trump is the most transparent leader to come along, according to some on the right, the media, Fox News notwithstanding, is reporting on that transparency...hence accurate reporting. Still, I believe the media is not reporting on some of the negative aspects of this administration enough.

Paul: Mike, the news you likely watch has 90%+ negative stories about Pres. Trump and you think that upping that % would be more accurate? Please share the % negative you think would be the "right" amount, in your opinion. If it doesn't burn your eyes, here's an article that might enlighten, if you let it do so.

As you can feel, the division is palpable and the condescension by some, continues on:

Mike: Paul, Washington Times? Yikes. Trump brings on the negative coverage because he does negative things. Read and watch the news then do a little research. If Trump is the most transparent leader to come along, according to some on the right, the media, Fox News notwithstanding, is reporting on that transparency...hence accurate reporting. Still, I believe the media is not reporting on some of the negative aspects of this administration enough.

Paul: Mike, again, not quite like a substantive rebuttal where you point out real inaccuracies that you might see. Looks like prejudice and ignorance based in fear of facing the facts to me.

Mike: Paul, how can I refute nothing? With nothing?

Paul: Mike, I suppose you'd have to put on your reading glasses and read the article and refute at least one point; fact against counter fact. Or you could just give your opinion on what percentage of negative reporting above 90% you think would be appropriate for President Trump.

Beth: I suggest you start by only discussing and debating articles that appear in the neutral, fact-based zone.

Paul: Beth, thanks for the chart and article. Does that mean for you that you disregard anything written in Mother Jones, The Huffington Post, or see on MSNBC (all on the skewed left side of the chart), or do you read with caution knowing that they have a slant?

Beth: Paul, not at all, it just means that the majority of stuff blasted about on both sides is highly biased, and you're over here posting links to one of those biased sources and asking people to refute it.

Paul: Beth, that a source has a bias doesn't mean it's wrong correct? The IPCC is hugely biased and I suspect you believe their reports. If you do, where's your consistency?

Mike: Paul, Beth, thanks for the chart and article. "Does that mean for you that you disregard anything written in Mother Jones, The Huffington Post, or see on MSNBC (all on the skewed left side of the chart), or do you read with caution knowing that they have a slant?" Read your own words!

Beth: Mike, funny how he is so hyper-focused on the left – rather than recognizing his own bias.

Mike: Beth, I noticed that.

Paul: Hey Moron, there's no secret that I'm a conservative. I'm asking for your own consistency. You're wanting me to disregard an article that you haven't bothered to read just because it is on the right side of the graph. I doubt that you only read or watch stuff that's only in the middle of that graph. We all have to weigh and use our judgment on anything we read or watch. But, you have to have judgement to use when you're doing that. I'm not clear that you have any and you aren't displaying much in this conversation.

Mike: uh oh, Paul has lost his cool. Just to be fair I did read that article. In my profession I have to instruct my students to know fact from fiction, so why would I change that tact in my private life? I also dive deep into issues and I do look at many points of view. I consider sources, I fact check, and I make sure what I post is accurate. And if I'm wrong, I own up to it. You wanted me to respond to the article? When I see conservative or liberal watchdog, I take what they say, put my own research on it and then I have my own spin.

As you can feel, the emotional intensity is heating

up and even a direct insult of "Hey Moron," was thrown in. In a dialogue like this, division often widens and not much is accomplished. As the social media thread continues, so does the frustration, emotional projection and name calling.

Paul: So Diane, Mike and Beth wadded into the question and either sank or squirmed. Any chance that you will boldly go where others have failed? As a reminder the question is, "how much more than 90+% negative reporting would be the correct/proper amount if what is currently being done isn't, in your opinion, sufficient or if you consider it balanced? Obviously, this is your discussion and you can go through the motions of inviting dialogue and then avoiding the actual heavy-lifting when your offer is accepted.

Diane Altomare: Paul, character matters. And character means, regardless of what people say about you, including the media, that you have the grace, humility and peaceful strength to stay focused on your purpose and mission and not attack people with vile comments, and dangerous slogans like 'fake news' or 'enemy of the people.' It is not becoming to the President of the United States and is a disgrace to this country and our democracy, that our president uses those slogans, as a way to attack the media. People say many negative things about me, all the time, and I will not lower myself to a low vibrational level of name calling, attacking and bullying to deflect attention from how it feels, make myself feel better in the moment, or make a point. Or worse, rally a bunch of people against another group of people, like our president does continuously. That's what bullies do on the playground in middle school. And even bullying on the playground in middle school has evolved, because there are programs and many people who realize how detrimental it is to individuals and to society, as a whole. Our president is trying to take us backwards. And for those of us, that see what is happening and how detrimental this is, we must continue to call out this disgraceful and unacceptable behavior.

Paul: Diane, for me to say that I find you a great pontificator but short on succinct responses to direct questions, is that an attack or a rude observation?

Alan: Problem is Trump lies 90% of the time. So you don't want news to report it? When he blames every problem he creates on Obama (is there a statute of limitations on blaming your predecessors?) when he says the tax cuts for the rich are for the middle class, when he says there are good

Nazis, when he says North Korea will denuclearize in a year, every day a new lie...yes, the media which he likes to call 'enemy of the people,' must report it. If you don't want to hear facts, just watch state run propaganda TV Fox News. When Trump creates trade wars with our allies, lies about why, says the democrats created his racist policies against immigrants, he should and is called out. When he says the Russia probe is a witch hunt even though there are 23 indictments and guilty pleas, he is lying. It's not a witch hunt, it's a probe to prosecute those who are committing treason!

Paul: Alan, almost nothing you wrote above is accurate. Does that mean you are lying? If you believe what you're saying it's not a lie, but it is a misstatement. President Trump said that he would move the U.S. Embassy from Tel Aviv to Jerusalem. Did he lie about that? He said that he would pull out of the Iran nuclear deal. Did he lie about that? He said that he would nominate judges to the Supreme Court who read the Constitution and apply its principles to present cases. Did he lie about that? He said that the Paris Climate Accord was a very bad deal and he would withdraw the United States from it. Did he lie about that? You may want to at least revise your percentage of "lies" you believe that President Trump has said so that you don't incriminate yourself; sort of like being hoisted on your own petard, isn't it?

Diane Altomare: How about you answer your own question Paul? You calling me a pontificator – or as it is defined as, "annoyingly pompous." Is that rude, an attack or you calling me names? And what is the intention of it...how is that helpful in anyway?

Paul: Diane, you wish to judge and criticize president Trump. I pointed out that the choice in November 2016 was between Trump and Clinton. You imply that Clinton was the better choice. I'm asking you to give your rationale for that implication. You're dodging the question and giving a lot of words which have nothing to do with it. I believe that I have correctly identified that as pontificating.

Diane Altomare: Paul, I did not imply Clinton was the better choice. I am not talking about and won't be talking about Hillary Clinton. I am focusing on what is happening right now in this country, with this president. My original question was "does character in a president matter anymore?" I'm not dodging any question. And so we are clear, I don't have to answer every question you ask. And I get to respond, in whatever way I want to. And just because I don't answer the way you want me to, it does not give you free reign to call me names. It's beyond pointless...and simply ends a conversation. But just because you end a conversation, by calling people names, doesn't mean you win. It actually means "no one wins" as we are all in this together.

Paul: Diane, you seem to be perplexed as to why one side of the divide supports Pres. Trump in spite of his character flaws. I'm telling you that, the many flaws in Hillary Clinton far outweighed the flaws in Donald J Trump. You choose not to look at that and that's up to you, but don't act like it's not there. I thought you wanted to learn something about the divide, but acting like that rationale is illegitimate is part of the divide. And you add to it by pontificating.

Alan: Paul, OK 89% of the time, yes he did follow through on some stupid campaign promises. Thank God he didn't build that stupid wall and have Mexico pay for it! Regarding the other stupid things he did follow thru on; getting out of climate change and Iran and trade deals with no replacement, shows he's a deal breaker not a deal maker. He's too lazy to actually create deals, much easier to break them. Anyway, what you pointed out covers the 10-11% of the dumb things he said he followed through with. The every day lies are too numerous to mention. Anyway, keep getting your news from Trump TV and vote against your own interests and you will be fine!

Diane Altomare: Absolutely not my truth Paul! Hillary Clinton has nothing to do with this conversation, at all. People can still support the president's policies, and at the same time call him out on his disgraceful behavior. It's that simple.

For those of you following along, that are interested in healing and embracing your shadows. When someone calls you a name, and let's just use "annoyingly pompous," as an example, because I was just called that on this thread. You have one of two options: you can either be affected by it, get defensive and attack the other person or you can use it to heal and emerge stronger and more whole. I choose the latter. So here's how this works: my work now is to embrace being "annoyingly pompous." And then anyone can call me that name or any variation of that, and it won't affect me. It will simply be a word that they are using to deflect their own fear, anger or hostility and it won't impact me in anyway. I will be sharing more about how to specifically do this, in my upcoming book.

Alan: Wow Diane, that book is perfect for our times. Way to actually practice it right before our eyes! Thank you for modeling that behavior. You helped me just today.

There is so much to be emotionally heated about. That is one thing we can all agree on. What's important is that we resist the urge to project that frustration and fear onto others. And as we continue to be inundated with new happenings and new reasons to be emotionally heated, that we continually make it a point to process through our emotional upset and tend to our well being. If we don't, emotional exhaustion is imminent.

EXHAUSTION OVERLOAD

The issues addressed in the social media threads thus far, are just a slice of what each of us is processing through and grappling with, daily. It's no wonder, so many of us are exhausted. However, we need to be very careful to transcend any exhaustion and stop fighting each other because this emotional exhaustion has the power to deplete our energy, tear us down and render us powerless.

Former GOP Political Strategist, Steve Schmidt, said on Bill Maher, "There are two ways to fight. One is to exhaust your opponent, so they

check out. You can bring your opponent into sub-
mission. Or you can break their will to fight. The
degree to which Trump and his lies and the con-
stancy of the craziness – it breaks peoples' wills. It
checks them out. They become exhausted by it."

Many have echoed Steve Schmidt's words and
many of us feel the exhaustion from all the chaos,
the heartbreaking issues we are facing, the President's tweet storms and the social media battles, like
you witnessed above.

One of my friends shared this exact sentiment
urging us to be cautious of this very exhaustion and
overwhelm:

*"Trump wants to keep us busy arguing about his lat-
est Tweet or comment made at a rally, while he continues to take serious action against our well being &
our nation's highest potential. He is a smooth opera-
tor, a con man.*

*Let us continue to speak our voice against the
matters that go against our moral compass and stop
our people & nation from thriving! Don't stop calling
representatives, sending post cards. Register family,
friends & co-workers. And have your voice speak the
loudest with your vote."*

Exhaustion and overwhelm are two defeating forces that can lead to an even greater sense of powerlessness. They threaten your ability to remain clear, confident and prepared to stand up for what you believe in.

If you have felt either exhausted or overwhelmed over the past few months, you are not alone. If either emotion is still present, close your eyes, get still and simply connect with this emotion.

Feel the exhaustion or overwhelm in your body.

Then give your emotion a voice.

The voice of your exhaustion may be saying, "You are depleted. Be diligent in taking care of yourself mentally and emotionally by honoring your feelings; by acknowledging that these are challenging times that require extra self care. Spend more time in meditation, connecting to yourself and your values. This will give you the energy, stamina and clarity you need to press on."

The voice of your overwhelm may be signaling, "Don't take it all on. Pick one or two issues that you feel passionate about. Speak out. Take action. Vote. Make a difference on these specific issues."

Finally, take action. What has the wisdom of your exhaustion or overwhelm guided you to do? Put it in your calendar and make a commitment to yourself, to do this.

It's essential to acknowledge that because we are inundated with so much breaking news every day, there is an exhaustion and overwhelm epidemic in our country that is as real, as all the tangible issues we are also faced with.

One of my friends shared how exhausted, she truly is:

I'm fed up with everything in government. I'm fed up with all sides. I'm fed up with the lies. I'm fed up with the lack of integrity. I'm just pretty pissed off in general. You know doing personal growth work, as a coach, I know that everything is a reflection of me, and I am a reflection of everything else. So when I start thinking about the anger, the division, the sense of entitlement, how we are in some cases putting band-aids on situations that really need some excavating...so that people can step up into their greatness, rather than continue in the thought process and the beliefs of being a victim and not having any opportunities. I trust that this is a break down to a breakthrough, but if there is a way that you could suggest we process our anger, process our fear and take some deep breaths, and maybe some appropriate action. I would sure love to know what action other than writing my senators or congressman would look like.

Olivia's question is a powerful one because although writing our representatives is absolutely essential, there's more we need to do to affect the change we desire. In addition, there's so much we can and must be doing to empower ourselves, instead of being at the whim of the feelings of powerlessness or resignation.

So what can we do besides writing our representatives? Pick one or two of these that resonate with you, and begin today:

- Take the hostility out of your relationships.
- Stop judging or insulting people that disagree with you politically.
- Require that people stop attacking you in conversations.
- Do things in your life that empower you.
- Get involved in groups that support what you believe in.
- Vote.
- Run for Office.
- Bring your unique contribution to your community.

- Process through your emotions when they arise.
- Communicate your views with clarity and compassion.
- Use this as the wake up call, it's intended to be.

Above all, ask yourself:

"What is something unique I bring to the issues our country is facing?"

Heed the answer you get to this question and take action. Go out into your community and share your greatness. Share who you are from a place of love. Help people around you.

Connect with what you're great at. It doesn't have to be focused on political issues, although it just may. However, by bringing more of your greatness, more love, more light, more joy, more positivity into the world, you are a solution to the division and the hatred that's present.

And if you want to affect things politically, there are so many groups that have started as a result of all this division. Find one that resonates with what you want to bring more of into the world and band together with others to create more light and love. Be a part of the change. Make your voice heard.

As a result of taking action, regardless of what ultimately happens, you will know that you used these challenging times as the impetus to grow, evolve and bring your greatest contribution to the world.

In the next chapter, we will identify inspiring ways to empower yourself and those around you.

6

REGAINING POWER

There's nothing more disconcerting then being gravely affected by something you have no control over. While there are times when we literally don't have the power to change what's happening, there are others when instead of exerting our power, we choose to stay mired in the anxiety, fear or chaos we feel.

One of the most effective ways to regain control over a situation or experience that's upsetting you or is in violation of your values, is to recognize that you have the power to do something. You have the power to choose. There is always a way to move beyond the upset, anxiety or fear and reframe the experience, in a way that empowers you to act and be part of the solution.

Choice is one of our freedoms in the United States of America. There are so many choices available to each of us, living in a democracy. And exerting your freedom to choose who you are, what you stand for and what you're willing to do to stay true to your values, at this time in our country's history, is imperative.

Our democracy is being attacked. Our Intelligence Community has unanimously stated, "that Russia is still meddling in our elections and this is not going away."

In addition, Director of National Intelligence Dan Coates stated, "We continue to see a campaign by Russia to try to divide the United States."

Unfortunately, Russia has already succeeded in dividing us. Our work now is to take back our projections and stop fighting each other, and instead listen to and honor each other's differing points of view.

Here's one way to do this. First, simply notice the moment you're judging someone for their political view. Remind yourself, that although what they believe may be in total opposition to what you think is right, each one of us comes from different circumstances, a different upbringing and sees the world through a different perspective. Instead of separating yourself from them or fighting against their way of thinking, choose to give them grace to feel the way they do.

It doesn't mean you have to agree with their political views or even like what they believe, it simply means you are choosing to not cast negative energy towards that person. It means allowing them to feel how they do, as you honor how you feel as well. It is the work of having compassion for each other. By accepting their views as they are, instead of depleting your energy fighting against them, you remain connected to your truth and your power.

It's not always easy to do, because the issues we are facing are emotionally impacting each one of us. But it's imperative to remove the judgment, hatred and name calling, and instead bring love, understanding and connection into our dialogue, so we can stop fighting each other, remain focused on the important issues and be prepared for what's ahead.

Although many of the issues we are facing are complex, or beyond the scope of what we feel we can individually affect, we must acknowledge our ability to affect change and never lose sight of our collective power as Americans to make a difference. Part of what's essential in upholding our democracy is speaking out and requiring change, when needed.

In the post below, I share my feelings about our

president's meeting at the Helsinki summit with Russian President, Vladimir Putin.

MY POST

What is happening? Our president is blaming the United States, our country...the country he is supposed to be leading, for poor relations with Russia, a country that is attacking us.

Donald Trump tweets last night, "Our relationship with Russia has NEVER been worse thanks to many years of U.S. foolishness and stupidity and now, the Rigged Witch Hunt!!"

It's time for us all to wake up, my fellow Americans! This is, our democracy. How do you feel about Trump's meeting with Putin?

SOCIAL MEDIA THREAD

John: So ashamed of that man we have as president. Self interest over America's interest? Disgraceful!

Molly: Blame on both sides? Same words he used to justify racist Neo Nazi actions. He is very intentional about his words and manipulations.

His words and actions today are nothing short of treason!

Barb: all I have to say – Obama's Apology Tour

John: The right likes to throw out the lie about the Obama's apology tour. Reread Obama's speeches dealing with foreign nations. Obama never said sorry but did speak truth on some U.S. past practices. But Obama never uttered support for a foreign power's interests over the interests of the USA. What Trump said today is treasonous and it is time you stop defending someone who won't defend the U.S.

Diane Altomare: No amount of distraction or manipulation can change what we all witnessed yesterday. Many of us knew that our president wasn't properly protecting our country against Russia. Our intelligence has consistently been clear about it. And now it is crystal clear to all of us, what is truly happening. Our president works for Russian interests, not American.

Rachel: Diane, I feel paralyzed over what we all witnessed yesterday. Now we know that Cult 45 is a treasonous traitor. I do not know what to do with this anxiety, other than meditate. Maybe I'll just drink a lot of wine and numb it all out for a few days.

Kevin: TRE45ON

Cynthia: I wonder where all the Trumpsters are today! Glad they're not trying to defend or explain away our disgraceful White House occupant's behavior yesterday. No surprise to me. He does not support this country or the diverse people who live here.

Carrie: Just the beginning. Our country is in terrible danger and the Republicans need to do something fast...they are selling out this country for the Supreme Court.

John: I noticed that a lot on the right rightfully defended our intelligence communities, but failed to hold Trump accountable for his words yesterday. It's time that they put America first when our president refuses to do so!

John: Let all of our representatives in Washington know that they need to hold Trump accountable. We The People deserve better!

Lauren: I'm making calls daily to my senators to let them know the behavior of this president on a global scale is abhorrent and must be condemned. It's so very simple to do and you don't even have to speak to anyone if you'd prefer not to – you can just leave a message. Dial the general number for your reps – (202) 224-3121. Thank you!

Regaining our power simply means that in the

moments we feel something is in direct violation to what we stand for as Americans, we speak out and take action. Instead of resigning to things staying as they are, we hold true to our values and allow our truth to inspire action.

One of my dear friends did just that. He wrote a letter to his congresswoman urging her to stand up against the president siding with Russia. He wanted to know what was being done to protect our democracy from Russian interference in our upcoming elections.

As I was writing this chapter, I received an email from him that said, *"I got a response from my local congresswoman!"* The senator's response to my friend Dan, was extremely thorough and gave specifics on exactly what Congress is doing to address his concerns about Russian interference in our 2016 presidential election, as well as future elections.

Not only is it imperative and effective to contact our representatives in Congress, it's part of what we must do to have our voice heard, regain connection to our power and be a part of the change.

Now more than ever, we must acknowledge that there is power in each one of us reaching out to our representatives individually and even more power, in our collective voice. Most importantly, we must utilize this power. Today, take action on an issue that you feel passionately about. Here is the general number to contact your representative in Congress: (202) 224-3121

Also, you can search for your representative and send them an email. Or you can use this app, which is how my friend Dan connected with his senator: https://resist.bot/

AMERICA SPEAKS UP

Another way, we as Americans have exerted our collective power and made a huge difference in many people's lives, is by speaking out and stopping the Administration's zero tolerance policy.

This policy that resulted in children being taken from their parents at the border, awakened intense feelings of outrage, upset, helplessness and powerlessness in many. But the barrage of emotional upset and outrage didn't stop the American people. It empowered us. Ultimately, we exerted our power and influence by using our voices to stand up, against this atrocity.

Although a few people in the post below represent Americans that stood in favor of the zero tolerance policy, fortunately enough Americans transformed their feelings of powerlessness and turned their outrage into action, speaking out against it and ultimately causing the president and his administration to reverse this policy.

MY POST

Bring these families back together! Law and order has prevailed in our country, as judge, Dana Sabraw orders families to be reunited, at the border. The judge called this a "chaotic circumstance of the governments' own making." And said, "this situation has reached a crisis level and officials had no real plan in place for reunification."

Let's pray that this administration knows where these kids are and can actually make this happen. Ruling: the Trump administration must reunite separated families within 30 days, and children under 5 must be reunited with their parents within 14 days. #FamiliesBelongTogether

SOCIAL MEDIA THREAD

Liz: Omg this is so so so sad! This is just beyond heartbreaking to me! My heart hurts for these families!

Kevin: The intellectual suicide of the left in this country over this issue causes me great pain, particularly when the cause of the problems are not made by the US government, but rather by people attempting to enter the U.S. illegally. What's the responsibility of the Mexican government for its citizens in all of this?

Jan: Seriously! Please drop the politics and return. I'm over it. The fact of the matter is laws get broken and families are separated. People break the law, are sent to jail, and are separated, so duh.

Diane Altomare: Absolutely not Jan! I will not turn my head away from the cruelty of this administration and what is happening in this country, emotionally and morally. I will continue to speak out and stand up for what I believe is aligned with the values of who I am and the America I love. And the beauty of the America, I know, is that we are each entitled to speak up and to express ourselves freely. There is nothing to "return to," we are being called to emotionally awaken, individually heal and emerge stronger together.

Cynthia: Really Jan! That is your response. Accidents happen, families get separated. When, where? Not since thousands of children were taken from Native Americans. Do you not have any compassion? This isn't about politics, it's about values, empathy, integrity and respect.

Peg: It's sad, that human dignity and respect is considered political. We can keep families together, give them due process and send them home and not treat them like animals. Treating families with empathy and compassion does not mean we think they have a right to stay. I said it before, Jack. These are not just ideological differences. These are differences in values and foundational character. I try to teach my children that every person deserves to be received with an open heart. That doesn't mean we owe them money, jobs or privileges, reserved for citizens. They have endured more pain than most of us will ever feel in our lifetimes. The indignant pleasure that some people enjoy by watching the plights of others saddens me. These are not people I want in my life.

Jack: So Peg, are you saying you agree with the lawless policy called "catch and release" or just that anyone with a child should be treated differently when they come across the border at something other than a regular port of entry (I'm assuming that you know that families aren't/weren't separated at established port of entry centers) where they could be processed. Have you gone through customs at an international airport? If people started running past you while you were standing in line and they seemed to get away with doing it, would you continue standing in line or would you break ranks and run the way they did? How is this different? So, if an individual did the line busting that person should be stopped, i.e. apprehend, but if an adult with a child did the line breaking they should be stopped for a moment and then sent on their way together? If you think that walking across our border is different than flying over it, please explain your rationale. Thanks.

Peg: Jack, I said no such thing. I said that they can be treated with dignity and respect without being afforded privileges reserved for citizens — as they were (with some exceptions) before the zero tolerance policy was instituted. I've been through customs at our ports dozens and dozens of times. I was born in Germany and lived in England for 3 years. We have many reasons to travel often. I'm not sure that walking over the border and flying to it are at all apples to apples. Anyone who flies here, or arrives by ship, can present themselves at that port and seek asylum. There are always exceptions, but a person flying here has some verifiable identification and at least the means to navigate getting out of where they were. An assumption on my part, but I assume that people presenting themselves at an international port tend to have more resources than the ones who risk their lives and the lives of their children by traveling underground. If they could do it a different way, they would. And, no I don't believe that dignity and empathy should be weighed depending on how someone arrives in front of you. Even the president decided that the policy was untenable and acted within his authority when Congress wouldn't stop the practice of separating parents and children. Similar to homeless populations, it's tough to accommodate adult men and women together. I get that. But allowing children to stay with mom, and older boys to stay with dad, and giving them daily access to speak to one another until we figure out how to send them home isn't exactly handing them the keys to a house in the Hamptons. We have an immigration crisis in this country. But we're better than taking an already downtrodden person and breaking them. Making sure families know where each member is while they go through the grueling process of deportation doesn't seem like offering a luxury to me.

Fortunately, the judge agreed with the many Americans that felt the zero tolerance policy was abhorrent and inhumane. It not only exemplifies the collective power we have in this country to affect change, but further shows what's possible when we reconnect to our values, speak out and take action.

Like the many Americans that turned their outrage into effective action to stop the zero tolerance policy, we always have access to a more empowering option than the one we are experiencing.

EXPRESSING YOUR TRUTH

This holds true for relationship issues as well. Many people feel disempowered by what's happening in their relationships. For many, speaking their truth and communicating their views isn't without complications or repercussions. I have heard this from many people, as I have dove into political conversations with people on both sides. Some have shared that their spouse disagrees with them politically and it's causing a strain on their marriage. Others say they are no longer talking to family members because they just don't see eye to eye and can't communicate calmly due to opposing political views. Because of the animosity that's present in some relationships, many people have chosen to remain silent about how they feel.

Unfortunately, when someone is not open to hearing a differing political view, there may be little you can do to communicate how you feel politically with that specific individual. Understanding that they may be too emotionally affected to have a healthy conversation, is the key to accepting their limitations.

A couple friends have shared this very experience:

My cousins have lost their ability to have compassion

*for others. I thought they had a heart. But now, I
can see how wrong I was about their character. We
simply don't value the same things, and it's pointless
talking about it. They don't listen. Unfortunately,
Trump being elected has put a rift in our relationship
that I'm not sure can ever be repaired. We just don't
talk to each other anymore.*

*My husband has no compassion for what others go
through. I truly didn't see how selfish and narcissistic
he was, until Trump was elected. It has put a huge
rift in our marriage, and he simply won't talk about
anything without shouting at me or calling me a lib-
tard, and telling me to stop watching 'Fake News'.
I'm not sure there's any turning back from here.*

Many people have relationships just like these, that
have been severed because of differing political
views and values. And some don't see a way to
regain connection with their friend, family member,
spouse or colleague.

However, there are relationships where having the
tough conversations and making attempts to heal
the rift is possible. And most importantly, in these
relationships, taking out the judgment and projec-

tion is necessary, in order to find a place of reconnection and peace.

I have two people in my life that I adore and are very important to me, who I strongly disagree with politically. However, I have chosen to not allow these intense political differences to color my view of who they are. And I'm grateful, they have done the same for me.

It is not always easy to understand why someone holds one value more sacred than the other. But that is what is required in our relationships, at this time in our country. We must dig deep and find the way to transcend the difficulties, disagreements and sometimes, drag out debates. We must hold steadfast to a knowing deep in our hearts, that each one of our relationships can transcend this difficult and divisive time.

In 10 years, when you look back at the relationships in your life that were threatened as a result of political differences, will you be able to say that you weathered this temporary storm?

Because that's what it is. It's temporary. And the depth of our relationships is much more powerful than this time in our history.

Here are a few guidelines to integrate into your

political conversations, to foster more harmony, compassion and ultimately, reconnection:

- First, it's essential to remain connected to your truth and your views.
- Second and just as important, be open to listening to and honoring how the other person feels, even if it's diametrically in opposition, to what's important to you.
- Third, remind yourself that in the United States of America, we share a powerful freedom: to have differing views and to express them freely.
- Fourth, set boundaries for your political conversations. Tone down the intense language. Leave out the insults or name calling. And require the other person does the same.
- Fifth, stay on topic. If the conversation gets off track, gently and lovingly redirect the conversation towards what you were originally talking about.

Above all, if at any time the conversation gets too heated or results in name calling or insulting, take a deep breath and give yourself permission to halt the dialogue until you can both come back to communicating with civility and grace. Practice communicating with these guidelines and don't expect perfection right out of the gate. Relationship harmony can take diligence and patience.

Over time, as you put these guidelines into practice, you may find that you are able to communicate more clearly and effectively, without shutting down or being as emotionally affected, as you may have been in the past.

Civil dialogue is the key to healthy relationships and to creating more harmony in our political conversations. It's not always easy, but it is worth it.

CLEAR, FIRM COMMUNICATION

Having civil conversations however, does not mean you have to abandon your values, or water down your views, in any way. It simply means that you choose to communicate your truth with love and grace.

In my work to communicate with people on both sides, there were many posts and conversations on social media that got heated, where I was being challenged and my views were being attacked. I also received emails from friends of mine that were critical of my intentions, and unclear as to why I was sharing my views in the first place.

In an effort to keep the peace with my friends, I could have easily made a decision to be politically neutral, instead of sharing how I truly felt. However, part of regaining our power is staying true to who we are, what we believe in and expressing our voice. In this interaction, my intention was to do just that.

Here's the email I received from a dear friend of mine:

"Hi Diane. I am passing this information video along because I thought you would find the information useful. In the interest of being truthful on your blog and having all your facts right, I thought you may want to listen to "the other side" from time to time. Your blogs and posts are very one sided and I think you have a responsibility to your listeners to hear both sides. I know of several of your followers who told me that they have either blocked you or unfollowed you because they feel that you are not educated enough about the other side of the argument to give unbiased opinions."

And here's what I shared with her:

"Thank you! I will definitely check it out. I am very

clear about the other side's views and feelings about many issues, but that doesn't mean that I agree with them. I am not trying to be unbiased, and people blocking me or unfollowing me, is because they can't just be with somebody having a different opinion, and that is OK. Part of healing the emotional divide, is being OK with other people's opinions, even when it triggers or affects us.

My intention in helping to heal the emotional divide in this country, is that we can get better at expressing how we feel, without attacking, belittling, labeling or calling each other names. My mission is that simple and although sharing my views may complicate that, it truly is the only way to do this authentically and with lasting impact."

Blocking, un-friending or unfollowing every one that disagrees with your political views, is not going to reunify us. What will bring us back together is what America stands for: honoring each other's point of view respectfully, even when we disagree. That is what this country and democracy was founded on and is spiritually, the only way to healing.

It's essential to remind ourselves that the most important thing we can do in these challenging times is to acknowledge how we are being emotion-ally affected and do the inner work to heal what's happening. Only then, can we truly come to these conversations with clarity and intention. And in addition, have the inner strength to stay true to who we are and what we believe in, while at the same time respecting another's point of view.

Regaining our power is simple, although it's not always easy to do. What it requires, is that we first reconnect to who we are, our truth and the values that are important to us. And ultimately, we use our deepest truth to summon up enough courage to speak out and take action for what we believe in.

In the next chapter, you will learn ways to reacti-vate and access a whole new level of courage.

REACTIVATING COURAGE

Extraordinary courage often arises from our deepest pain. On the flip side, the inability to act courageously often means we simply haven't yet connected with an inspiring enough reason, to do something beyond our comfort zone. Something that would catapult us into extraordinary action.

In the post below, I share my heartbreak about the children in detention centers at the border and how this very heartbreak has driven me to continually speak out about this atrocity and contact my representatives in Congress.

MY POST

When I was a little girl, we used to drive from

the suburbs into the city of Chicago every Sunday to have Sunday dinner with my grandparents. I remember driving through the projects in Chicago, where even as a young girl I could see how differently the little girls and boys lived there. I remember thinking how unfair it seemed to be. And the one question that permeated my mind back then was, "Why me...why do I get to have all that I do, while these other little girls and boys live in broken down buildings with raggedy clothes?" It has always deeply affected me to see this disparity in life. I feel the same way today, as I did as a little girl, as I hear the stories of these children in detention centers, without their parents. This is an atrocity happening here "on American soil," as Kirsten Gillibrand tweeted this morning.

Americans, we have a heart and it is our responsibility to not grow weary and continue to speak out and take action. We each must decide what we are willing to do. What is one action you will take today?

Senator Kirsten Gillibrand's tweet: The nightmare of the Trump administration's inhumane border policy is still unfolding. Hundreds of children are still being held in detention facilities, wondering: "What about me?" As many as 500 of these children's parents have already been deported.

A public health official warned the Trump administration of the harm its family separation policy would cause to these children. It was told of the trauma it would inflict and the lasting psychological damage it would do. The administration went ahead with the policy anyway.

Reports of abuse linger around some facilities. We've heard stories of children being sexually assaulted or forced to take psychotropic drugs. Stories of children being returned to their families sick, beaten or emotionally distressed. This is happening here, on American soil.

I'm asking you to be the hope these families came for. Keep speaking out. Keep donating to organizations offering them legal aid and counseling. Keep calling Congress to demand accountability. We have to stay by their side, today and for as long as they need us.

SOCIAL MEDIA THREAD

Ashley: Amen! We must correct this wrong. We, who have our heart strings being pulled by this horrible action must be their voice and call this inhumane act what it is: wrong. Thank you to all who care, want better and are doing everything they can to bring forth change and better in our nation. We are all here, at this time, for a reason.

Jill: Thank you, Diane! I had the same experience as a small child riding the bus from the Indianapolis suburbs with my mother, going through the old slums of the inner city before we came to the pretty stores. My heart just broke open and has never stopped hurting. The people were raggedy and dirty and looked so hungry...so lonely and forsaken. I always asked myself the same question you asked "why them and not me?" We are meant to be the helpers.

The heartbreak I felt as a little girl and still feel about people that are suffering, drives me to do extraordinary things; things I normally wouldn't. Writing this book is one of those. This subject matter has not been easy to write about. There have been many moments I've had to dive deep and summon a whole new level of courage, to write what I needed to express.

My old programming and shadow beliefs to "keep the peace" and "be a people pleaser," have been challenged many times in my deeper commitment to communicate how I feel about what's happening in this country.

They have been challenged by some people urging me to stop speaking out, because it is in opposition to what they believe or makes them feel uncomfortable.

This comment I received from one of my friends criticizing my work to heal the emotional divide, challenged my shadow belief to "keep the peace" and required that I both reconnect to my courage and in addition, my inspiration for doing this work. Here's part of what she said:

"I personally think you are creating more division than you are creating healing, but that is just my opinion."

Here's what I shared with her, on social media:

"How am I creating more division by expressing how I feel? It is not my responsibility to tend to others' emotional upset. What is my calling, is to teach and lead ways to heal our inner emotional upset so that we can respect each other, deeply and wholly."

What are your thoughts on what I'm sharing and how it's impacting you?

SOCIAL MEDIA THREAD

Julia: You're not responsible for how other people feel about your opinions, needs, wants – anything. You deliver each of these things with compassion and kindness, which is all we can ask for in the way we relate to one another. Good for you, standing with your calling...you're helping more than you are dividing.

Jane: Love it!

Michelle: You may not be responsible for how others feel, but I don't feel people can learn from you because it's obvious, you've picked a side. It feels like what I view is wrong, because I'm not on your side.

Maybe, if you understood my side and posted something acknowledging how I feel and why, I could relate more.

Diane Altomare: Thank you Michelle for sharing how you feel. I completely honor your point of view and respect how you feel. Although, I am sharing how I feel, it doesn't negate your view of things, in any way. That is the black-and-white thinking that we must rise above, in order to transcend our differences and be able to lovingly agree to disagree.

I have not picked a side. I am simply sharing my

views on different issues. And more importantly, I have never once said you are wrong or need to change, if you don't agree with my view. I have actually said the opposite. My whole intent is to foster healthy communication so that we can each express exactly how we feel, even if wildly opposing, and even if we are intensely emotionally affected. And at the same time, we can lovingly agree to disagree and remain friends. I believe this is possible and have many people I love, that strongly disagree with me and yet we still love each other. That is the ultimate goal.

Jessica: The divisions are already out there, you are not creating them, you describe them, you express your thoughts and feelings as everyone has a right to do, I don't think you are creating the divisions nor contributing towards more.

Melissa: Diane, I have a tremendous amount of respect for you, for how you are guiding the process of respectful communication.

I've watched you become a target for those who do not agree with your political positions because they are being emotionally triggered. I've also noticed that you NEVER make them wrong for having a different opinion than yours. They just feel like you are.

It seems that the point to this sometimes painful

process is to stand your ground in your beliefs, to not let people bash you with shame or hurtful behavior, and to teach others how to identify and manage their darker shadows.

You have helped me with your consistent gentle style, and for that I am grateful. Keep it up. We still have a long way to go!

Brenda: Diane Altomare, I think you have been very committed to allowing everyone to express themselves and still very honest about where you stand. Unlike you, I have come to the opinion that all the conversation doesn't really get us anywhere. Trump would be a dictator if he could get away with it. He is a liar and a racist and the truth is he doesn't care about anyone, but himself. He made lots of promises to coal workers that he could never keep. Now saying there were laws about separating families. Another lie, all he had to do was make a phone call. Everyone is dug in to their perception and talking does not seem to shift this. We have a civil divide in this country and it's about values not parties. Trump was pro life, friends with the Clintons, not religious, cheated on every wife he had. He is a fake and in our white house. It's a disgrace that he is representing this country. The people supporting him don't care what he does. They believe he will solve all their problems. He is only working on behalf of the wealthy. I don't know how to talk to someone who does not see this. It would be like when Hitler was voted in and then became a dictator. No one believed the things that were being done. We all know that story. It feels the same to me. All the fear mongering is being aimed at people of color and Muslims. I do not see how this situation can heal.

Before we continue on with ways to reactivate your courage, it's important to address what Brenda just shared in the previous comment, because resigning to accepting circumstances that we feel are out of our control, can drain our energy and keep us from connecting with the very reason or vision that will awaken the courage we need to move forward.

Nonetheless, I know that many can relate to her feelings of hopelessness. Many of us have felt this way, or may still have the belief that we can't heal this divide. But as a coach and healer for the past two decades, I've seen the most irreparable relationships heal and people transform in the most profound ways. And more importantly, I believe there is a divine purpose we are experiencing this darkness: for the sole purpose of healing and evolution.

Whether you are spiritual or not, this is what evolution is. It is the purging of the old, for the new.

The sifting out of what no longer works, for what does. And in the transition of any change, there is pain. That pain is what we are in the grips of right now, in this country. And we each have the opportunity to choose how we will respond.

Like NY times bestselling author Dr. Wayne Dyer said, "when you are squeezed, what comes out is what's within." We are each being squeezed right now, by our neighbors, our friends and by family members that disagree with us politically, and we have to choose who we are and who we are willing to be. Are we going to respond with hatred and insults? Or are we going to dive within to heal the emotional upset that's arising and evolve more peaceful and able to bring kindness, love and solutions to the issues, our nation is grappling with?

It truly is an individual decision each of us must make, sometimes on a moment by moment basis. And it's not a decision to take lightly, as the collective outcome will be determined by what each one of us chooses to do.

So how exactly do we do this? By embracing both the light and the dark shadows, within.

THE DARK SIDE

"Anything we judge is our shadow," says Debbie Ford, NY times bestselling author of *The Dark Side of The Light Chasers*.

You can start embracing your shadows by simply identifying what you have judged your spouse, friend, colleague or parents for.

Maybe you have called one of them:

- emotional
- arrogant
- sensitive
- weak
- angry
- mean
- hateful
- a racist
- a bully
- a snowflake

Remember, we are all every quality we see others' exemplifying. By embracing this quality within ourselves, we are less emotionally affected by it and more able to understand when someone acts out that quality or shadow, that they're often being driven to do so unconsciously. Then in that moment, instead of being a victim to someone's shadow self playing out, we are able to witness what's occurring and respond with clarity, instead of reacting emotionally.

Another dark shadow to explore is the one that may be keeping you from speaking out, communicating your truth or contributing your unique gift to the world.

Maybe your shadow is:

- not good enough
- not smart enough
- too old
- scared
- unable to communicate eloquently
- a people pleaser

The brilliance of embracing any dark shadow is that through connection and communication with these parts of you, you make peace with the very shadows that hold you back from expressing yourself authentically.

I embraced many shadows, in the moments I was being affected by people's responses to what I was sharing on social media.

Embracing My Pompous Shadow

As I shared in chapter five, one of the specific names and shadows I was called in one of the social media political conversations, was 'annoyingly pompous.' How did I know it was one of my shadows? Because in the moment I read his comment that said, "you are annoyingly pompous," I was affected by it. It bothered me. I thought, "How can he say that about me? I'm an expert. I'm not being annoyingly pompous." And in that moment, because I was getting defensive, I knew it was a shadow I needed to embrace. Here's how I made peace with the annoyingly pompous part of me.

First, I acknowledged the quality exists within me.
By simply breathing into connection with the truth that there are times I can be 'annoyingly pompous,' I was on the road to releasing my attachment to it.

Sometimes, it can be hard to connect with qualities that we have judged or have been told are wrong or bad. However, by acknowledging and embracing these qualities, it means you will be more neutral about this part of you, as well as this part or aspect in others. By embracing 'annoyingly pompous,' it will be both ok for me to act this way at times, and I will be less affected when someone else is acting that way, as well.

Second, I identified the gift of this quality.
I recalled a few times in my life when being 'annoyingly pompous' had served me. Actually, there were many. As a workshop leader, it has always been essential to be powerfully rooted in my convictions and truth. When someone may feel resistance to what I'm sharing or question my expertise, having the ability to stand true to my knowing is essential.

Remember, all of these qualities are subjective. What I may deem confident or convicted to a specific truth or knowing, someone else may call 'annoyingly pompous' or 'arrogant' like I experienced with my friend, that called me this name on the post.

Third, I embraced this quality by going within.
I closed my eyes, took a deep breath and connected with the annoyingly pompous part of me. I visualized what I've looked like in moments I've been 'annoyingly pompous' and I reconnected deeply with the times this quality served me. I spent a few moments, simply honoring and embracing the 'annoyingly pompous' part of me without judgment.

Fourth, I said "I am that" out loud.

I embraced and owned this quality by saying out loud, "*I am annoyingly pompous and I love myself completely. It's ok to be all that I am.*"

The brilliance of embracing 'annoyingly pompous' is that I don't have to hold back my authentic nature in an effort to mask my confidence or expertise in any specific area, for fear of somebody thinking, I'm too much of this, or too much of that. I can say exactly what I want to express and know that however people choose to respond, is coming from their perspective and doesn't have anything to do with what I'm communicating.

Now it's your turn. Take a moment to jot down your answers to these questions:

- *What have I been judging others for?*
- *What name or names have I been called on social media or in political conversations that have put me on the defensive or hurt my feelings?*

These are your shadows. Take a moment to pick one of these for the exercise below.

For example, let's look at the shadow, selfish. Maybe you felt angry last week at dinner, because you felt your friends were being selfish. You were upset with them for not giving more attention to the atrocities that are taking place with others, and instead selfishly focusing on their personal financial gain and the booming economy. Let's look at how you can embrace this shadow.

First, acknowledge this quality exists within you.
Close your eyes and simply breathe into connection with the selfish part of you. Selfish can be a tough shadow to embrace for martyrs or people pleasers because they are often taught that there's no circumstance, when being selfish is ok. But remember, by acknowledging and embracing this quality, it means you will be more neutral. It will be both ok for you to 'be selfish' at times and you will be less affected, when someone else is selfish.

Second, identify the gift of this quality.
Recall a time in your life when being selfish has served you. Or when you needed to be selfish to take better care of yourself, and you weren't able to do so.

Third, embrace this quality by going within.
Close your eyes and breathe into connection with

the selfish part of you. Visualize what you've looked like in moments you've been selfish and reconnect deeply with the times this quality has served you. For a moment, just honor and embrace the selfish part of you, without judgment.

Fourth, say "I am that" out loud.

Embrace and own this quality by saying out loud, *"I am selfish and I love myself completely. It's ok to be all that I am."*

Remember, our goal in embracing our shadows is not to eliminate any quality or on the flip side, exemplify it's characteristics intensely. It is to be neutral. It is simply to be ok in the moments that 'you are that.' When we aren't at peace with a quality that exists within us, we are driven to prove we are the opposite and that's when our shadow self acts out inappropriately, creating chaos or other challenges in our lives. These are the moments when we get defensive, insult others or lash out at people on social media. And it's the same, when the president attacks people on Twitter or at his rallies.

We have seen Donald Trump's shadows acting out intensely, over the past two years. One of his biggest shadows is insecurity. And of course, this is a quality we all possess and a shadow for many of us, as well. Remember, when we can't allow ourselves to be something, we will go to lengths to prove we are the opposite.

So what does the president do when he doesn't want to appear insecure or weak? He makes a point to prove how confident and secure he is, especially in the moments he's being criticized or called to account.

Numerous times in tweets and press briefings, he has declared, "I am a very stable, genius."

One, was in response to a reporter asking him if he would be contradicting himself once he boarded Air Force One and began tweeting. And this tweet by the president, was in response to the release of Michael Wolf's book, *Fire and Fury*, that depicted the president in a bad light:

> "*Actually, throughout my life, my two greatest assets have been mental stability and being, like, really smart*," said the President. "*Crooked Hillary Clinton also played these cards very hard and, as everyone knows, went down in flames. I went from VERY successful businessman, to top T.V. Star ... to President of the United States (on my first try). I think that would qualify as not smart, but genius ... and a very stable genius at that!*"

You may be wondering at this point how the most powerful man in the world could be 'insecure,' and moreover, why we would we want him to have the capacity to exude his insecurity? Very simply, because he is human and we are all everything; we each possess every quality there is. And ironically, as is the case with all of our shadows, our inability to be a specific quality allows that very aspect to control us. Trump's inability to be insecure, forces him to have to always act as if he is confident and strong. And many would argue that he spends an inordinate amount of time doing this, especially on Twitter.

If the president didn't have to prove how confident and secure he is to cover up his shadow of insecurity, he wouldn't spend so much time on Twitter getting defensive, bashing people or calling people derogatory names. As of this writing, he has attacked and insulted 487 individuals and institutions. That's an extraordinary amount of time spent, trying to cover up his shadows.

In addition, Trump's inability to admit when he is insecure or uncertain about something, ends up being a weakness, because in the end this very shadow could keep him from seeking advice or learning something new. If he wasn't so driven by the unconscious need to prove he isn't 'insecure,' he could admit when he didn't know or understand something. Instead of agreeing with opposing sides and creating confusion in a meeting on immigration, for example, he could learn something he needed to know, to make an informed decision.

The true peace and strength he could exude by embracing his shadows, instead of allowing them to lead his actions and our country, is immense. And the same is true, for each one of us. Instead of arguing or attacking others on social media and instead of separating ourselves from people that disagree with us, by embracing our shadows and acknowledging we each have the capacity to exude every human quality there is, we are ultimately less emotionally affected by what's happening and more able to focus on the many issues that need our immediate attention.

Now, that we've spent some time on the dark side, let's go to the light.

THE LIGHT SIDE

By embracing our light shadows, we are more equipped with love, confidence, strength, light, joy, and peace. Pick a quality from the list below that would support you in activating more courage in your life or something you want to experience more of.

Maybe you could use a little more:

- uniqueness
- courage
- power
- boldness
- eloquence
- clarity

First, acknowledge this quality exists within you.
Close your eyes and simply breathe into connection with this part of you.

Second, identify the gift of this quality.
Recall a time in your life when this quality has served you.

Third, embrace this quality by going within.
Close your eyes and breathe into connection with this part of you. Visualize what you've looked like in moments you've exemplified this quality and reconnect deeply with the times this quality has served you. For a moment, just honor and embrace it without judgment.

Fourth, say "I am that" out loud.

Embrace and own this quality by saying out loud, *"I am ___ and I love myself completely. I embrace all that I am."*

By acknowledging that you are everything you see in the external world and embracing each quality wholeheartedly, you free yourself from being controlled or driven by any one aspect of the human psyche.

The gift of embracing your shadows gives you the ability to allow others to be who they are, without being weakened by what they are doing or saying and reconnects you to the depth of who you are, including your capacity to act courageously.

In the next chapter, we will explore ways to respond peacefully in any circumstance, experience or conversation, regardless of the emotional upset that may be present.

8

RESPONDING
PEACEFULLY

A peaceful response to any conversation or circumstance is only possible when we are grounded and
centered in love. One of the main reasons people
are responding with anger, hostility and insults is
because they are deeply connected to the intensity
of their emotions and thus, reacting emotionally.

As we have been exploring, both processing
through your emotions and embracing your shadows will bring you to a grounded, calm state where
you can communicate intentionally, with clarity and
grace. Here's a visual to use in any moment you feel
a conversation getting heated.

FULL PROOF CIRCLE TECHNIQUE

Imagine standing in front of the person you're having a conversation with. Now take an imaginary piece of chalk and draw a small circle between the two of you. Picture that every time you have a negative judgment about this person, every time you lash out or insult them, every time you say something negative or judgmental about them or to them, every time you hold onto a resentment and choose to not forgive them for what they've done or said, negative energy goes into the circle of space between you and the space gets wider and deeper. The small circle eventually gets bigger and bigger creating a larger separation between the two of you; pushing you farther apart.

Now look down at the circle and notice that the circle is not only touching your toes, it's touching the other person's toes, as well. Whatever you put in this circle is going to eventually come back to you. If you lash out with anger, if you throw insults, if you are snarky or condescending, that negative energy will circle back around and you'll be touched by it, in some way.

By becoming conscious of what you're putting into the circle and making simple, immediate adjustments to what you are bringing into your conversations, it helps you become more conscious and intentional with your communication. In addition, if you say something unkind or hurt someone, you have the opportunity to clean it up; to acknowledge that you didn't mean for it to be hurtful. By doing this, you are removing the negative energy in the circle between the two of you.

This visual illustrates how and why the divide in our country has been widening. Many continue to put negative energy into the circle, with name calling, attacking, being less than civil or outright hostile.

Instead, use this visual to decide what you want the outcome of your conversation to be. When you don't see eye to eye with your spouse, in-laws, one of your parents or colleagues, and you feel the conversation turning sideways or heading for disaster, this will give you the few moments you may need to shift your focus and be intentional about what you want to put in the circle, between the two of you.

Here are a few questions to ask yourself, to discern whether what you're saying or doing will ultimately bring you what you want:

- *What is my intention for this conversation?*

- *What do I want more of?*
- *What can I do or say to bring more of what I want to experience in this circle, between us?*

Above all, be gentle with yourself and others. Getting to relationship harmony and changing what's happening in our current conversations is a process.

Not only is it possible to change the way we are communicating with each other, but I have witnessed it occur. There are numerous times in healing the emotional divide, that I have been able to vividly see the progress we are making.

In this post, I again brought up the atrocious policy of kids being separated from their parents at the border. In the past, the conversation about this issue had gotten heated and quickly gone off the rails. But this time, civil conversation was possible because just about everyone responded from a place of kindness and compassion, instead of attacking each other.

MY POST

Thank you Jacob Soboroff for calling out the president, with your tweet this morning:

"You, only you, systematically separated kids

171

from their parents — in many cases possibly permanently — and put them alone in cages.

I saw them. No excusing Obama, Bush nor Clinton who started deterrence policy.

But you alone are the architect of kids-in-cages-as-deterrent."

The fact that Donald Trump is talking about the comparison of media coverage of immigration policies, between him and Obama, is disgraceful. He is totally missing the point. More than 2000 children are separated from their parents. But he continues, to try and deflect people's attention from these children, and put it on him.

We will not turn our attention away from what's important, Mr. President.

SOCIAL MEDIA THREAD

Michael: DJT hate speech has been unprecedented. He is immoral and his actions are indefensible. This is not some simple left or right debate. Mexican immigrants are murderers. Muslim travel ban was his initial action. Obama was born in Kenya and needs to prove. Imprisoning children because parents ask for asylum. Wow! How can anybody defend this?

Tony: Won't be looking to you for any objective summary of the president's remarks.

Michael: I agree I am not objective against the onslaught of vile hatred from our president. I am sorry for my emotions. I am not proud of it.

Tony: Michael, awareness is the beginning of change. That's true for all of us. In the interchange with those with whom I disagree, I see parts of me that need changing. That's part of the benefit of honest internet dialogue. The chance of us meeting is slim, but here we are communicating. I love this country for making this possible.

Diane Altomare: Michael, you don't need to apologize for feeling emotional. Emotions are a part of being a healthy human being. And emotions are valuable to us; they are messengers that can signal that something is not OK with who we are, what we believe in or what we value. Processing through these emotions in a healthy way is important, so we can come to any conversation with intention and clarity, instead of projecting our emotional upset onto each other.

Martin: Tony, I appreciate what you said about seeing interchange as a way to improve.

Martin: Sometimes processing emotions means expressing them loudly. Is that unhealthy? There is never a time when the expression of emotions is bad. It is only the way that they are expressed that can be damaging and I didn't hear anything wrong with your expression Michael.

This dialogue, where people found a way to connect instead of attacking each other, is the kind we need more of.

What made this possible? Mainly Michael's decision to be vulnerable and share his truth when he said, "I agree that I am not objective against the onslaught of vile hatred from our president." In that moment, instead of attacking Tony for commenting that he 'clearly didn't have objectivity,' Michael agreed and shared the reasons he simply couldn't be objective. He shared his truth and his heart. This very moment changed the tone of this conversation from one where divineness and hostility had been present in the past, to a peaceful conversation where each person shared how they felt and what they were experiencing and grappling with. It's important to note that although Michael went on to apologize for being emotional, all emotions are valid and there is never a need to apologize for how we feel.

Although this post went well, there are many others that haven't. Let's break down what often keeps us from responding peacefully and civilly.

There are three main reasons we don't or can't have a civil, political conversation with someone:

1. Unresolved emotions
2. Past trauma
3. Responding from our wounded self

We've been talking a lot about unresolved emotions and how to process through them and ultimately, transcend their intensity. Let's now look at how your wounded self keeps you from the peaceful dialogue you desire. Remember:

Our wounded self is the part of us that holds onto repressed emotions, unresolved events and painful relationships from our past.

Each one of us has had experiences in the past, that have been painful. And because we didn't have the support or understanding to process through those emotions, they became wounds that we carried into our adult life.

Then in the moment somebody insults your intelligence in a political conversation for example, by saying, "you obviously don't have the intellect to discern the real truth," your wounded self wakes up. Because your Dad used to call you stupid when you didn't do things he wanted you to, their insult unconsciously triggers that unresolved hurt and wound.

In that moment, instead of responding from your grounded, calm self; from a place of clarity and intention, you may react defensively, deflecting the attention from your pain or upset, by attacking or insulting the other person in return.

This is often a natural human tendency when our wounded self is affected. We either insult the other person as a way to deflect how we are feeling or we may separate ourselves from this person because they are triggering our old wounds. The alternative and ideal option which we've been talking much about, is to use it as an opportunity to process through unresolved emotions, past trauma and ultimately, heal.

One way to consciously arrive at this ideal choice is to first realize when the opportunity to heal, presents itself. There's a simple way to determine when a healing opportunity is present. Simply notice when you are pointing the finger at somebody else, and attacking or insulting them instead of focusing on how you feel. Use this as a signal that there's an unresolved emotion that needs processing or a shadow that needs to be embraced.

Also, it's important to note that there are times

when we are being affected by something and it's OK, and even imperative to respond from our emotional guidance.

The distinction lies in whether you first process through your emotional upset, or instead project that emotional upset onto the other person.

Our emotions are messengers. They are here to guide us and signal what we need to do or say to be in integrity with who we are and what we believe in.

Remember all the times I have called the president out for name calling, labeling and insulting others? This is absolutely originating from my emotional guidance. It is being driven by the emotional upset I feel when I hear the president demeaning the integrity and respect of the office, and acting like a bully on a playground.

It is similar, for example, to you feeling angry or upset because your child is being bullied at school. By processing through your emotional upset first, you gain clarity to know exactly how to handle the situation from a place of love and grace. Then by communicating with your child's teacher or principal, you are calling out the behavior of this bully and protecting your child from this unacceptable attack on their self esteem.

Because there is no teacher or principal to contact regarding the president's name calling, bullying and labeling, we must first process through our emotional upset and then come together, to call it out.

In the post below, I did just that.

MY POST

Our president is a master at dividing with his fear mongering, name calling and insults. He talks about people like he's a part of the "mean girl" crowd in high school at his rallies, and gets people riled up to hate each other. His view is: one side against the other. This is a low vibrational way of being and is permeating our country, and it has dangerous implications. This bullying is not ok and demeaning to who we are as Americans. Ask yourself, "am I against or angry at people who don't agree with me politically?"

I see people attack others, who don't support this president's playground bullying tactics. For what? Do you not think this is negatively impacting the civility in this country?

We have to begin healing this divide by listening to each other's feelings and hearts, instead of defending the presidents' hateful words.

Of course, you can be a conservative and believe strongly in your views. I agree in some conservative policies, but will never defend a president who name calls, labels, insults and bullies people...who calls our media, "the enemy of the people." It is against the love and respect I stand for, at the depth of my being.

Brian Karem, Executive Editor of Sentinel Newspapers said, "Words have consequences. Words have meaning."

We have got to wake up and stop fighting against each other. Five journalists were killed yesterday. And whether you strongly believe, it is one of the implications of Trump's intense attacks on the media, or whether you believe that's ridiculous...the fact remains that we have to make some significant changes in ourselves and the way we relate to others, that disagree with our views.

Important note: All views are welcome here. Healing the emotional divide, is not about trying to change somebody's view politically. It is simply, being able to have a conversation with people that have differing political views (or different values) than you, with love, respect and compassion. To allow each other to be heard without attacking, name calling or labeling – to not project the intensity of your anger or upset onto that other person, but to listen and to be heard. So that we can begin to heal the emotional divide and come back together again.

SOCIAL MEDIA THREAD

Todd: A civil war doesn't happen if no one shows up. There are darker forces trying to divide us. Don't feed them.

Diane Altomare: It's not a matter of whether we feed the dark forces. What we have to do is bring light to the darkness, and call it out. We each have darkness within us, that we need to tend to and this is an emotional awakening for us, to each do this individual healing work. We simply can't turn our heads away from what's happening, and declare that by not acknowledging it, it means were not "feeding it." I understand what you are saying Todd, however we still have to have the courage to call it out, and heal the ways within each one of us, that we are a part of and are contributing to this dark energy. I'm calling it out. And that's very different, than feeding it.

Todd: I agree on the individual healing work, in fact that is all we have. We apparently can't communicate civilly on social fronts because no one is listening to the other. Righteous indignation will be our downfall. Transcendence above this political sideshow bullshit is the answer. I don't care if you voted for Trump or Hillary, I will like you or dislike you based on your heart and your soul, not who you voted for. Besides, we haven't had a real leader since Kennedy or Reagan...Yes, I love them both...and they tried to call out the dark forces, and they both received bullets. It's ludicrous how we can get behind either party. They are a distracting side show.

Ray: I happen to think Obama was a great leader in spite of a congress who's main priority was to make him a one term president and to vote no on almost everything. He stayed above it. Never went to childish name calling; family was a model for elegance and still got a lot done. You may disagree and that's ok too.

Todd: I totally agree.

Jenna: Very low vibrating energy indeed. People have become emboldened to say exactly what's on their mind. There's no grace or room for difference of opinion anymore. Indulgence in our negativity only creates more of the same.

Ray: When they go low, we can still go high. When they want to meet in the middle, we can have a civil conversation with opposing views. When they go hate, racist and attack I will defend!

David: There also has to be a willingness on both sides to listen. If we are more concerned with making our point and winning than hearing the other side, then we end up with both sides feeling unheard. With that being said there is also a point where hearing the other side doesn't matter because what they are doing and saying is so horrible or detestable there is no reason to listen. Not sure where we are on that right now.

Diane Altomare: David, I feel it's just messy right now. But we have to be willing to continue to have conversations with people that have opposing views. And do it in a way, that is kind, loving and compassionate. I see people making progress in ways, in the conversations we've been having. Some are able to at least hear each other, and then others, just can't listen because things are too emotional.

David: Sometimes when I listen they say things that are hurtful and toxic in a public forum. I draw a line when I reach out from love and compassion and have the door slammed in my face. I no longer stand as a punching bag for those on the right who only want to condemn and fight. My time is worth more than that. I remember a wise woman telling me when she spoke that she never expected the whole audience to like her or be willing to listen, so she spoke to those who would listen. I am speaking to those who will listen because I know the truth will always win.

Diane Altomare: Yes, I have had the exact same experience David, being a punching bag to others projections of anger, hatred and frustration. It truly shows me how much people need to embrace their shadows and process through emotional upset, right now.

Let's do this. Take something or someone you are being emotionally affected by and transform it into the insight, clarity and guidance you need.

First, notice something you are upset about and identify specifically, how it makes you feel.

Maybe you feel anger, anxiety, fear, sadness, or helplessness.

Simply breathe into connection with this emotion and give it a voice. You can listen to the wisdom of your emotion, by asking yourself:

"What is the voice of this emotion trying to communicate or guide me to do?"

Maybe the voice of your helplessness is screaming, "This isn't ok. How can this be happening?"

Maybe the voice of your sadness is saying to you,

"What has happened to our country? I can't believe this is taking place in the United States of America. It breaks my heart."

The voice of your fear may be signaling, "I can't imagine what life would be like in the United States of America, if we were no longer a democracy. Is this actually possible? What can I do to be a part of protecting the democracy, I have grown to know and love so dearly?"

Remember, by giving our emotions a voice, two things happen. First, we begin to connect more deeply with how we feel. By doing this, the emotion begins to lose its control and the intensity of it diminishes. Second, we gain the insight of our emotion. This very insight often directs us toward the action we need to take to move beyond the emotional intensity we are feeling, and begin creating more of what we want.

Most importantly, once you have gained the insightful wisdom your emotion has for you, take action. Take an action that's aligned with what you want more of in your relationships, your community, your life and our country.

What Peace Is Not

Let's talk about what responding peacefully is not. Responding peacefully doesn't mean that you don't share your truth. It also doesn't mean that you are always responding from a place of joy or happiness.

Sometimes responding peacefully requires that you are firm and vividly clear about what's important to you, who you are and what you value. Sometimes responding peacefully is coming from an intensely impassioned place. It is absolutely possible to respond peacefully, while at the same time being firm and convicted in your truth.

Here is a post I shared, where I was peacefully responding to someone bullying, insulting and attacking me on a different social media thread. Even though my words weren't fluffy, light or 'feel good' words, they were coming from an impassioned place of clarity and self truth.

My post

Truth be told: You can label me and call me, any name you want. It doesn't change what I'm saying or how I feel about what I'm sharing or the views I'm expressing. Many people have labeled me and called me many names, over the past few months, as we've been courageously having these very tough conversations.

It doesn't scare me or force me to be quiet. If you are labeling people or calling people names, it just makes you somebody, that insults people, like our president does.

We each have to be accountable for how we are treating each other. And regardless of how you feel about what I'm sharing, I still choose to respect and honor your view, even if I strongly disagree with it.

SOCIAL MEDIA THREAD

Andy: ...but names will never hurt me...Brava!

Jenn: Well said!

Catherine: Good for you. Real leadership!

Emily: You give me hope.

Adam: I remember a wise woman once saying that if up to 30% of people don't hate you, you're not doing it right.

Erin: Keep speaking up, sister! We are listening and with you!

David: Likewise, you're a great person and I honorably call you friend!

Liz: Your wisdom is immeasurable. I like to hear

what you have to say. On the other hand, this world is filled with bullies who serve little value.

Denise: His job, may or may not suit him, but as my president, he owes it to all of us to speak respectfully to those who he represents, as an immigrants son himself...our USA flourishes with diversity and that's a good thing, both here and around the world.

Responding peacefully is exactly what this country needs more of. Take some time today to connect with others and communicate in a way that both honors who you are, and at the same time allows you to express your truth with grace and kindness.

9

FORGING AHEAD POWERFULLY

The fate of our country and democracy, as well as the impact this division will have on our future, has yet to be fully determined. Each of our decisions and actions will be part of creating, whatever is yet to come. And yes collectively, we as Americans do have that much of an impact on what happens to our country, moving forward.

For this very reason, it has never been more imperative that we decide who we are and what we are going to contribute to the America we hold dear and want to leave for future generations. Complacency is no longer an option.

Part of forging ahead powerfully is being clear on

the stakes. The other part is making an individual commitment to be part of the change, we desperately want to see.

The stakes are definitely high for many reasons, and on many issues. One that is of utmost importance and on the forefront of many people's minds is our democracy. Many Americans, including former government officials and journalists, have likened Donald Trump to a dictator.

Here are a few statements from the president that emulate a dictator style of leadership. Many center around the president's attack on our free press:

"The Fake News hates me saying that they are the Enemy of the People only because they know it's TRUE. I am providing a great service by explaining this to the American People. They purposely cause great division & distrust. They can also cause War! They are very dangerous & sick!"

"Just remember, what you are seeing and what you are reading is not what's happening. Just stick with us, don't believe the crap you see from these people, the fake news."

"So funny to watch the Fake News, especially

NBC and CNN. They are fighting hard to downplay the deal with North Korea. 500 days ago they would have 'begged' for this deal — looked like war would break out. Our Country's biggest enemy is the Fake News so easily promulgated by fools!"

Here are a couple comments from friends who are concerned:

"If you start calling a free press the 'Enemy of the People,' you have become the enemy."

"I have to say that I am usually a hopeful person but the state of the country seems beyond healing this divide. We have put up with the lying and insanity coming from the WH but this issue with these children being pulled from their parents is beyond anything a person would ever imagine happening in this country. I feel like I am living in Germany when Hitler became a dictator!"

Here are a few tweets and comments from journalists that warn the American people that the ten-

dency of dictators is to attack the press, and deni-
grate or dehumanize people:

John Avlon, CNN Political Analyst said, *"FDR
famously said the presidency is primarily a place of
moral leadership. This president is not trying to be a
moral leader in any way, shape or form. And that den-
igrates the office. And when you use the bully pulpit to
dehumanize your critics, that is uniquely dangerous as
history also shows us, really clearly. And that's why this
matters."*

Carl Bernstein, journalist and author, said on
Anderson Cooper, about the president threatening to revoke more security clearances, *"This is
what dictators do. This is a dictatorial exercise of power
that should frighten and call on all Republicans, to
say Mr. President you cannot do this. You are trying to
inhibit the free speech of people who may be in opposition to you, but they have a right to express themselves.
This is an act of authoritarianism and demagoguery
which defines who Donald Trump is. And his total disregard for the first amendment, as we have seen when
he calls the press, 'the enemies of the people.' Now the
national security and intelligence bureaucracy that has
served the nation well through the last 20 to 25 years is
also being called, in essence an enemy of the people, by
a president whose actions are inimical to the interest of*

the people of this country. *And this is noise to distract from his own inimical conduct and behavior, which is beyond anything we have seen from any president of the United States, certainly in my lifetime, including Richard Nixon."*

Jim Acosta, CNN Chief White House Correspondent tweeted, after it was suggested that his press credentials be revoked, *"Dictatorships take away press credentials. Not democracies."*

Lesley Stahl of CBS News recalls what Trump said on why he attacks the press, *"I do it to discredit you all & demean you all, so when you write negative stories about me, no one will believe you."*

David Gergen, Former Presidential adviser to Nixon, Ford, Reagan & Clinton said, *"Trump goes after his critics to silence them and punish them."*

Brian Stelter, host of Reliable Sources, said in response to Trump when he tweeted 'the media is this country's greatest enemy,' *"It is no wonder why most Americans think this president is not fit to serve. Tweets like this, suggest that he doesn't know what has made America so great for over 200 years and that is the check and balance system: between the exec-*

utive, judiciary, and the press. I think we should recognize how extreme his rhetoric is on this."

One of the world's most renowned journalists, Dan Rather, tweeted, *"We can't shrug off Trump's attacks on the press. Ever. They're undemocratic and invite, even incite, violence. This bears repeating. It demands repeating. Last night, CNN journalist Jim Acosta, faced down a hostile crowd. Support from his colleagues, competitors, and general public is a must."*

And here are a few comments from former National Intelligence officials, that again remind Americans, what this president is doing and why it's dangerous to our democracy:

General Michael Hayden, former CIA and NSA director, said to Anderson Cooper about the president revoking John Brennan's security clearance and stating other intelligence officials' security clearances, are currently under review, *"That was a threat that was put out there from the WH press room; in essence we're under review and that's simply telling us we are all being watched; we need to be careful. And one final thing, and this is the one that really matters. The White House just messaged the entire Intelligence Community, if you stand* up and say things that upset the president, or with which he disagrees, he will punish you. And that is a horrible message to be sending to folks who are there to tell you objective truth."

This statement, signed by 175 former senior intelligence officials, in regards to President Trump, revoking John Brennan's security clearance, "the president's action regarding John Brennan and the threats of similar action against other formal officials have nothing to do with who should and should not hold security clearances and everything to do with an attempt to stifle free speech. Decisions on security clearances should be based on national security concerns and not political views."

In addition, many Americans have been referring to "1984," a novel by George Orwell that described a dystopia where independent thought was suppressed, under a totalitarian regime.

Here's a quote from George Orwell's book, that's beginning to sound too familiar:

"The Party told you to reject the evidence of your eyes and ears. It was their final, most essential command."

Being able to criticize the president or call out

behavior that's inconsistent with our democracy and values we hold dear, is as American as the Statue of Liberty and apple pie. It's a must. As Theodore Roosevelt stated:

"To announce that there must be no criticism of the president, or that we are to stand by the president, right or wrong, is not only unpatriotic and servile, but is morally treasonable to the American public."

So where does this leave the fate of our democracy and the freedoms we have grown accustomed to? This will be determined by what we as Americans decide to do. And if you believe we're being led by a president that has authoritarian or dictator tendencies, the time to speak out, stand up and get involved is now.

So what does forging ahead powerfully look like, given the stakes and the issues we're facing?

1. When you feel something is in opposition to what you value or what America stands for, speak out and take action.
2. Gather with people that believe in the issues that are important to you and again, take action.

3. Vote.
4. Run for office.
5. And equally essential, tend to your emotional and physical well being, daily.

EMOTIONAL EXHAUSTION

One of the things that threatens our ability to proceed forward in a powerful way is that many of us are exhausted by the breaking news, happenings and events occurring on a daily basis. It's hard to keep up with, and at times, emotionally draining.

Let's look at a few ways to powerfully forge ahead, despite the emotional exhaustion and chaos.

First, realize that your well-being is one of the most important things you must tend to every day.

Second, acknowledge that it's essential for not only your well being, but for our democracy, that you don't become so exhausted that you stop speaking out or taking action.

Remember Steve Schmidt's powerful words? "There are two ways to fight and one is to exhaust your opponent and break their will to fight."

Not only have I felt total exhaustion at times, but I often hear others, refer to this emotional exhaustion as well:

"I'm so weary of being attacked by conservatives for standing up for the rights of these poor children, who are being used as a pawn. I'm shutting down today. I can't take it anymore."

"I simply can't handle it, so I'm just tuning it all out."

It's important to keep a barometer on how you are doing emotionally, as well as employ tactics to keep the exhaustion from draining you or breaking you down.

Be Intentional

One effective way to stay focused on what's most important is to be intentional about where you are directing your energy. It can be challenging in these chaotic times, as there is so much than can distract your attention, from any one focus. However, it is of the upmost importance on a daily basis, to work on staying focused on both what you value and what your priorities are.

And more specifically, how you can integrate watching or reading news coverage, assimilating what's happening and taking action to be a part of the change, with an already full schedule and life.

There are two things to focus on here.

First, your daily structure. It's important to be conscious of what you need to accomplish each day, while also integrating, the specific things you need to do to take immaculate care of yourself and your well being. For example, incorporating activities like exercise, meditation or eating well.

Second, put limits on what you will allow into your consciousness on a daily basis, balancing out the good and the bad. It's detrimental to our emotional well being to allow an overload of negative news or information to permeate our psyche on any given day. The cumulative effect of negative news seeping in day after day can take a toll on our well being, physically, mentally and emotionally.

What's most essential for you to gauge is your individual threshold. Where is the line for you? What is the threshold you have to be cautious of not crossing; where too much negative input is beyond what you can process through, each day?

Remember, a huge part of being able to allow any input of negative or upsetting news into your consciousness is by balancing it out, using the tools we've talked about. Ensure that you are processing through and able to transcend any emotional upset that arises, as soon as you are conscious, it's present.

When I was thick in the heat of people attacking me on social media, on the varying posts calling out the president, my emotions were high and shadows were being provoked. Throughout those months, I made a very concerted effort to check in and tend to my emotional upset, embrace any shadows and take care of my well being. It was essential to not only be able to respond from a clear, centered space but ensure that none of the negativity that was directed at me, was entering my consciousness or weakening me, in any way.

How To Stop Arguing

Another way to protect your energy and emotional well being is to learn how to powerfully and grace-fully share your political views without engaging in any low vibrational street fighting, especially in the moments someone may be goading you, into responding to their condescending comments.

In this post, you will see the difference between people that are simply sharing their views, wanting to engage in dialogue and others that insult, attack or are only interested in proving, that they're right.

MY POST

I'd like to address another one of the huge misconceptions, I encounter on a daily basis. Here's what someone shared with me yesterday:

"I think it is unfortunate that you attribute this all to Trump. Actually what I think has been overlooked is that this all has been brewing for a very long time. Trump is the voice of many middle American people who are so frustrated with being mummed by those who push their fringe exaggerated beliefs on everyone else. The quiet forgotten middle class is tired of being pushed out and shut up. They may not agree with everything he says and does, but they know he is in their corner fighting for them."

What I shared with her:

"I don't attribute everything to Trump and I do believe this emotional awakening has been simmering underneath the surface, for a long time. His behavior is disgraceful and that I am calling out. However, the emotional upset that has been awakened in each one of us as a result of this Presidency, is a spiritual opportunity for us to do the inner work to heal, and emerge stronger and more whole."

And on a side note, can someone, who is in the middle class, please explain to me what this Trump presidency has done, to not just make you "feel" like Trump is in your corner fighting for you, as my friend shared, but has actually given you a better life over the past 18 months. Because what I see on both sides, is many people who are fearful, angry and outraged and taking that emotional upset out on each other.

SOCIAL MEDIA THREAD

Jessie: Trump is a glaring symptom of the underbelly of the dark forces that break down our democracy and everything that makes America great. I just don't understand why everyone cannot see this. The rest of the world does!

These threads are not arguing about policies, but about how we can better respond to fear and rage. This is about how Trump shows up in the world, the way he tears down and insults others, the way he fights, and the way he bullies. It's about how all of this is affecting everyone. Trump's behavior is not ok and it is dividing the country and threatening our safety.

Eric: Trump is stopping the legislation by judicial fiat from SCOTUS by nominating judges who see their jobs as interpretation of the Constitution and not doing what feels right in the moment of any situation. We elected him to do that with every pick and not just his first one.

Helen: Possibly our constitution was relevant when it was written...and now needs some changing. All documents are subject to interpretation as well. Of course, the court is only as good as its judges, who are human and are often partial to a specific agenda. I don't think the "every man for himself" interpretation serves our country any longer. I could say a lot more, but fundamentalist devotion to the constitution just as to the Bible, has lead to extremism. For me this specifically applies to gay marriage, abortion, and corporations being treated like people. Eisenhower warned about the Military Industrial Complex...very wise man.

Eric: Helen, I hear you speaking from your fear and from a lack of information. It leads you to make proposals that are unwise, unsound and straight up violations of American values. This is why Diane and you are being opposed by people who wish to "preserve, protect, and defend" the Constitution. We have a process by which to make changes to our Constitution, but Progressives have instead used the courts and unelected judges to foist their will on the whole nation. If you're at all confused as to why Donald J Trump is in the White House instead of Hillary Rodham Clinton, look no further than that tactic which the majority of the electorate wishes to see stopped. For instance, if SCOTUS vacated the Roe v Wade decision, it wouldn't be the end of abortions in our country. Individual states, like CA, NY, WA, OR and others would see no change as state laws would prevail. All suggestions otherwise is propaganda and hype. If the Constitution doesn't unite us as a diverse people, full-on war may eventually be inevitable until we reach a resolution. No one wants that outcome and it's steadily moving in that direction.

In defense of the Bible, a fundamentalist reading of it includes "love your enemies" and do good to those who despitefully use you. Clearly violations of those principles are taking place with bible-believing people. But my understanding of people on the left is that they value tolerance and inclusion and I see an awful lot of intolerance and exclusion going on from that side of the discussions. It's hard to be true to our principles, isn't it?

Grant: Eric, you know darn well Trump and his ilk do not care for the constitution. Please stop the preserving the constitution argument you sputter out. This administration has had day after day of constitutional crisis. Just be real.

Eric: Grant, you are a very poor mind reader as I don't know that Pres. Trump doesn't care about the Constitution. Sounds like a projection on your part, straight up.

Grant: Eric you are a poor judge of character, straight up!

Diane Altomare: Here's a question, for everyone that excuses Trumps' name calling, labeling and bullying: "Does character in a president matter to you, anymore?"

Grant: Diane Altomare, yes.

Eric: Diane Altomare, unfortunately your question is a foolish one, as that wasn't the choice we had in 2016. The choice we had was between Hillary Rodham Clinton who is a known liar and now after the election, complainer and blamer of everybody but herself. You want to call that a woman of character? Perhaps you could tell me what accomplishment you look to that she did either as first lady or as Secretary of State, that you think qualified her to be president over Donald Trump? In presidential elections, we have to choose the best of the available options and not try to vote for something that doesn't exist. If Jesus runs for office in 2020, I'll vote for him over Trump.

Eric: Grant, now you have confirmed my initial judgment; I'm quite convinced you can't read my mind or intuit my intentions correctly.

Grant: Diane Altomare, we have to focus on the midterms and making our lives better each and every day. We can't reach those that choose to not listen to reason. We must convince those that have not chosen. I'm with you Diane.

Helen: Eric...please do not attempt to demean my opinion by relegating it to fear and lack of information. I repeat, there can be no strict adherence to any document written and interpreted by humans, as they are imperfect. I find it interesting how conservatives want to keep the government out of people's lives and choices except when it comes to telling women what they can and cannot do with their bodies, as well as who we are free to love and marry. When you talk about American values just what are you referring to? The right to poison thousands of children in Flint, Michigan with no consequences for those politicians who knowingly did this to save money? The right of allowing corporations to buy off politicians? The right of health insurance and big pharma executives to earn upward of 50 million a year? Oh yes, let's not forget "family values" when most conservatives only care about saving a fetus...when one in five children live below the poverty level. So what are these wonderful American values you speak of?

Helen: Eric, I find it interesting how your comments seem to drift into undermining the intelligence of those who disagree with you. The constitution isn't worth the paper it is written on, when it is interpreted and used as a means of keeping people in their place by rewarding the rich and powerful by giving corporations the status and rights of people.

Eric: Helen, I thought you wanted to keep this conversation civil but if you'd like to be snarky I can do that with you. While the governor of MI was a Republican, the city of Flint was run by Democrats and they made the decision to change the water delivery arrangements. The EPA, a leftist dominated agency, sat on the knowledge that Flint's water was tainted for over a year without taking action to warn and protect those affected people. So, I'm accurate to say that you are ignorant about those facts. I'm sorry if it upsets you to be schooled publicly by me in this way, but you chose the venue and style of the conversation. I can go into American values at another time as I think you have had sufficient schooling in this session.

Helen: Your condescension is not civil discourse...

Eric: Helen, but yours is? We've had thoughtful conversations before. I'm willing to meet you where you wish to take the conversation. I was accurate in assessing your comments to be uninformed and you took exception to that assessment. You could have ignored what you considered to be "just my opinion" but instead got defensive and began to double down on your ignorance. You can learn, even if it is in a painful lesson, get defensive and stay ignorant, or just go about blissfully disconnected from reality talking about how the divide between us can be "fixed" by destroying our founding documents. In the name of honesty, you could self-identify as a radical leftist who wants to use psychological language to lull to sleep those who want peace at almost any price.

Grant: Helen, Eric is one of those we cut bait on. He argues with nothing and expects people to refute that.

Eric: Grant, good thing you warned her to stay away as her discernment capabilities are certainly in question.

Diane Altomare: Eric, why do you feel compelled to insult people, as a part of these conversations? It doesn't help your arguments in any way, and is exactly what I have been calling the president out for doing and the reason we are having this conversation, in the first place. People are allowed to have their opinions, without you agreeing on every point. If what someone says offends you, or affects you in anyway, do the inner work to heal the anger, upset or frustration you are feeling. And then respond from a place of civility and kindness or simply, don't respond.

Grant: Diane Altomare, I know some of my digs get out, but I try hard to keep it level headed. I appreciate you holding people accountable for their words and actions, including our president!

Diane Altomare: Yes, it is something that each one of us needs to work on Grant! It's not always easy to stop the insult that is about to slip out or the dig that is coming from a place of anger or frustration. I admire your ability to acknowledge those moments when that happens, and then tend to your anger, fear or frustration.

Eric: Diane, thanks for the free instruction on how I might better "win friends and influence people." But by focusing on me it allows you to dodge the question I'm pointedly asking you, right?

Grant: geez, give it up Eric. Maybe the question is one that is just not a good...question?

Eric: Grant, that's your opinion. Are you Diane's protector or something? Do you view her as some damsel in distress who can't handle her own battles? The way you said that you were stepping out of this discussion, but keep jumping back in looks rather sexist to me.

Diane Altomare: Eric, what are you even talking about right now? The whole point of this conversation, on this page...is to heal the emotional divide. Which requires that we each look at how we are individually being emotionally affected by the conversations we are having. So we can stop projecting our fear, anger and hatred onto each other. We all need to focus on ourselves individually.

While there is some civil dialogue happening here, it is difficult for some in the post to refrain from personal attacks, jabs and insults.

This social media thread continued and unfortunately, it got even more personal. What it exemplifies, is the projection that's clearly taking place. You can feel the moments someone gets defensive and instead of dealing with that emotional upset, they lash out at the one they disagree with. The inability to have a civil conversation without personal attacks, name calling and labeling is part of what creates emotional exhaustion and is certainly a huge part of what's widening the division in our country.

SOCIAL MEDIA THREAD CONTINUES

Ian: Eric, the Flint situation is tragic. It's easy and partisan just to try to blame democrats and ignore the facts. Governor Snyder had a hand in it, as well as state officials, state appointed emergency managers, the county of Genesee, as well as the local city council. So instead of calling the EPA, a leftist organization because they are trying to regulate keeping poison out of our water, air and food, let's take a deep breath. Scott Pruitt is the head of the EPA and is deregulating poisons going into the Great Lakes, deregulating air pollution -allowing all types of poisons to be spread in our food supply; so hardly sounds like a leftist organization to me. But I am sensing this cannot be a discussion that will get anywhere, so just wanted to help with some facts. It's not all black and white.

Eric: Ian, the way you use inflammatory rhetoric and then accuse me of being incapable of civil conversation is just like what I have come to expect from people on the left. You speak peace and tolerance while steam rolling over any opposition. That Pres. Trump isn't listening to that kind of bullying is refreshing to those who love the rule of law over the rule of the mob.

Ian: Sounds like projection Eric.

Eric: Ian, I'm sure it does.

Eric: Ian, I know Diane and I don't know you. You've butted into this discussion as though you think she can't handle anything but admiration. Go ahead and be annoying and when I swat at you as I would a mosquito call it "hate."

Ian: Oh sorry, if you did not want anyone to address your inflammatory comments you should have DM her. She is perfectly capable of handling anything on her own. You are the one that keeps implying she needs help, not anyone else. So if you are concerned about anyone's comments, either don't post publicly or be able to handle alternate opinions. Thanks.

Eric: Ian, I'll block you if you continue to be annoying. It's as a friend that I give her criticism that would make her more effective in her stated mission.

Ian: Seems like you can't handle anyone who disagrees with you. I understand it's easier to stay in your Trump/Fox bubble than to hear facts. Feel free to block me. I'm not really interested in debating a guy who is so thin skin he attacks, but is scared to hear anything outside his own bias and non-fact based opinions. Weird you don't understand this is a public page not a private one, but ok.

Grant: Eric, sorry back in. Some friend you are. You are mistaking helping her. You write a lot but say nothing. Diane has stated her point of view and you just won't accept it. She calls out people who are morally bankrupt and are supposed to be our leaders. Her approach is exactly what we need. Your tact in this matter is exactly why we need Diane's voice.

Eric: Ian, if this is typical of the dialogue you have with those who disagree with your ideas, it must come as a shock that I continue to speak up here. You are being a total jerk because you don't like what I've said. You attack me personally, as opposed to confronting the ideas I've presented. So far you've done nothing to advance the discussion and have offered no substantive rebuttal to what I've written. If you think that resorting next to trading insults is what will be beneficial go right ahead, it's what I would expect from a guy of your caliber.

Ian: Interesting you call me a jerk and say I'm name calling. No response needed, you said it all!

Eric: Ian, I'm sorry, I meant to say fraud.

Ian: Have a nice nite, Eric.

Eric: Ian, if you don't mean it, don't say it?

Ian: Nite!

Sheila: As always, I appreciate your efforts to bring in valuable dialogue. When I see "slashing" remarks from people who have a "faith based" stance and review their argument, I'm blown away with inability to recognize history, their own privileges, and to focus so hard to prove their view without maybe sitting down to truly listen and have love and compassion for others. This is how a divided society breaks down and we do have history to validate our concerns. The saying 'what you focus on you'll find' can also be the toxins that keep people stuck and angry. Keep working to have a safe place to be.

While it's easy to get triggered by the lack of civility, names you may have been called or the unfair fighting or bullying tactics many of us have experienced in these political conversations, there is a huge opportunity in the midst of this very emotional upset; an opportunity to use it to dive within and tend to your emotional upset, embrace another

213

shadow, heal and emerge stronger. What you will see as you do this emotional healing, is you will become stronger, more focused and more able to remain clear enough to face what's yet to come, with grace, strength and clarity.

Here are a few guidelines to use when sharing your views and engaging in conversations, that will ensure you don't get too emotionally charged, don't get pulled into negative, demeaning dialogue and can remain clear and calm.

1. **Pay attention to how you feel.** Notice when you start to feel emotionally charged, whether it's a pit in your stomach, your fists start to tighten or you feel tightness in your chest. Honor your emotions and process through any emotional upset, before responding in any way.

2. **Be conscious of what may be happening for others.** Notice the moment someone goes on the defensive. You can usually tell, because they begin to insult, become sarcastic, condescending or use divisive language or labels.

3. **Above all, remain committed to taking care of yourself and your well-being.** There is no conversation worth, inciting

more stress or anxiety within you. Use whatever emotions arise, as an opportunity to heal.

Forging ahead powerfully requires that we each tend to our well being, process through any emotional upset that arises, and remain diligent in being intentional and focused on what matters most. (If you want to explore additional ways to transcend emotional upset and transform relationship chaos, I recommend reading my book *Clarity*.)

In the next chapter, we will explore ways to heal relationships, reconnect with others and ultimately, heal the emotional divide.

10

THE
RECONNECT

Lincoln: "A house divided against itself cannot stand."

So how do we heal the division and come together again? Simply by reconnecting to each other, one heart connection and one conversation at a time.

Early on in the writing of this manuscript and at the height of many of the social media conversations that were unhinged and going off the rails, this arrived in my consciousness in the wee hours of the morning:

I believe there is a part of us that wants to embrace the other side. That's curious. And almost magnetically pulled to explore why we are so different. Otherwise, we would stay segregated, divided and in separate camps –

we would re-organize and not communicate at all. Let's expand on this curiosity; this human need to talk it out, to debate, to even battle it out at times. So we can find that sense of wholeness again.

And after all the work I've done to heal the emotional divide, I still find this to be true.

I know it's true because I genuinely believe in the goodness of people. I believe many of us have a desire to gracefully navigate our way through these turbulent times. And that our ultimate state of peace and happiness is in connection to all people and all things.

In addition, as I've witnessed people both battling it out with each other and at times having civil conversations, I have felt this truth permeating through as the very reason, they were dialoguing in the first place. On the flip side, there are many people whose ego is driving them to these political conversations because they are uncomfortable when people disagree with their views or they simply want to prove they are right. However, there are many more people that are deeply concerned about the divide in this country and believe that despite our differences, we can find our way back to connection and unity again.

In this post, where I share that I will never be ok

with the name calling and lack of civility from this president, there are people from both sides weighing in. This conversation wasn't as heated, as some of the others have been. It is a powerful example of how we can lovingly agree to disagree and remain friends. It doesn't mean we will ever, all agree on issues or policies, but truly exemplifies that we can co-exist peacefully. And I'll take it. That's definite progress.

MY POST

Truth be told: I'm still not and will never be ok with this way of treating others, regardless of what someone is trying to accomplish.

This is what we are talking about on this week's show and I'd love to hear how you feel about the name calling and the way the president verbally attacks people. And in addition, whether his behavior has given other people permission, to do the same. Some agree with me, and some don't. I welcome how you feel.

Has all of this heightened the political discourse in this country?

Has the way the president calls people names,

made it fair game for everyone to have less civility and kindness towards each other?

In my quest to connect with all sides and help heal the emotional divide, I have experienced a level of intense anger being directed towards me, because I am calling the president out on this behavior. People being vicious and attacking what I'm expressing, which I understand, as they may feel I am against the president.

Except the truth is, I am genuinely expressing my disagreement with name calling and bullying others, verses attacking the president's politics or policies. I am expressing my intolerance of the leader of the United States belittling others and modeling this behavior for other people, to follow. I believe there is a difference and this distinction is important for each one of us to recognize, when we are communicating with each other. We need to separate who the president is being, from his politics and policies. It's ok to either support or not support his policies and at the same time, say you don't like how he calls people names, doesn't apologize and bullies people. It's ok to say, I'm not ok with the name calling, being mean or bullying others.

Here is an important question for each of us, to answer: Is the way the president's leading and what he is modeling, making it OK to be mean or hostile towards other people?

And just as importantly, can we all talk about this, without attacking each other or getting defensive? As attacking and being defensive are two different sides of the same coin of division and separation. Neither create connection or healing. They both divide and separate.

SOCIAL MEDIA THREAD

Sarah: This past year I have changed. After reading this, I will try to do better.

Diane Altomare: Thank you so much for sharing this Sarah! We have all changed in ways as a result of this past year, and this is truly an opportunity for each of us to learn so much about who we are, what we stand for, what is important to us and what we are going to bring to this country each and every day from this point forward.

Sarah: I feel angry that our government policies are changing negatively...EPA, Healthcare, Americans ignoring our leaders behavior and lack of obligation to all people. That the USA will no longer be known as the peacemakers of the world.

I'm so mad I've been ignoring my religious

beliefs. I want peace in my heart. Everyday it seems there is something else to worry about.

I want to be positive again and smile again.

Diane Altomare: Sarah, that is one of the gifts of all of this, which is to honor how we are feeling and what we are experiencing. To pay attention to what is most affecting us and know there is a message in it. To reconnect with what's important to you, what fills you up, what makes you feel good, positive, happy and whole again. I hope you will join us on tomorrow's show...we will be talking more about all of this.

Claire: My goodness! Lots of heavy duty stuff. I haven't been following. I am sad to read that you are being attacked. That is wrong and uncalled for. There is a very ugly attitude from both sides.

Diane Altomare: Yes, Claire. It's truly intense and sometimes very shocking, the way people respond with so much anger and hatred. However, it truly is an opportunity for all of us to be conscious of this emotional awakening and use it as the gift that it is intended to be: to evolve and create loving, peaceful lasting change.

Christina: There is a whole lot of cognitive dissonance going on...hanging on tightly to their point of view at all costs, so they don't have to feel uncomfortable through change.

Stephanie: Christina, maybe people have a right to resist change that they believe will harm their lives. I think many of us sit in judgement when we haven't walked in the shoes of others.

Diane Altomare: Yes Christina! And it's one of the most important reasons for us to open up this dialogue. To be able to see someone else's point of view and disarm the defensiveness and the attacking, so we can very simply talk and allow each other the space to be heard.

Natalie: Stephanie, you are right. People are afraid. And they're being given even more bad information to make them more fearful. It takes a lot of courage to turn away and place your faith in an unfamiliar direction with no guarantees. Many feel just too scared or exhausted to even try.

Lea: Love that you're taking this on. What I'm also seeing and experiencing is a waking up from political slumber. We're being shaken awake. That's a good thing. Maybe more will use their power and vote their conscience...whatever that is. We've been on autopilot for too long.

Diane Altomare: Natalie, I am absolutely seeing this and of course feel it, at times, as well, like you shared "being scared or too exhausted." It absolutely takes courage and that is what is needed to press on and stand up for what we each believe in. It is so important to do right now! Thank you for being a part of this essential conversation.

Heather: Need specific examples of name calling and bullying.

Diane Altomare: We will be talking about a few on the show tomorrow, Heather.

Mark: Never do you mention what the president does well or has changed. You know, the 63 million others who voted for change and see it. That side is very proud and happy and as his approval rating rises, we are all just blind? No one on the left will ever see that CBS, ABC, CNN, CNBC, and all the liberal stations really do the most bullying and attacking. Many times when we call someone a liar, bully, rude, name caller, and attacking, you just became the very person your pointing at. In doing so, as when you point, there are three fingers pointed back at you. We can agree that the personality of Trump, uggggghh, surely I did not vote for that, the policy change absolutely! Love and doing what you can for your country, the main thing to me and respecting the views of others, of course.

Diane Altomare: Thank you Mark. Can't wait to discuss this further on tomorrow's show. There is no easy answer and both sides have their views, which is why we need to continue to talk about this. And I so agree, when we are pointing the finger at somebody, there are three fingers pointing back at us – and always an opportunity, to look at our own behavior and who we are being. Which is the huge gift of the Trump presidency. For us to continually look at who we are being and at the same time, what we are allowing from others around us.

Because being complicit and allowing someone to behave in a disgraceful manner and still backing them, means that we are a part of that very hatred and cruelty. We have to look at our own behavior, when the three fingers are pointing back at us and we also have to look at what we are allowing from others. This president does not represent the kind of leadership that I believe in and I require more from the President of the United States.

I stand for love, compassion, kindness and all of us coming together again, even when we disagree. There is so much for all of us to learn from what we are experiencing.

Mark: I know but to calm everyone, look at the wonderful country we have under all presidents, yet poverty in every country, addiction too, crime as well, mankind is a deprived state of pure joy!

Claire: Mark – I so agree with all you expressed here. I did not vote for President Trump, my choice was Ted Cruz or any of the other Republicans. I agree that his personality is difficult to take and has said offensive things, yet I see many things I like very much in his administration and prefer to have someone who's personality is disagreeable, but gets it right on matters of national security and foreign policy. His decision on Iran is right on, his decision on moving the embassy to Jerusalem also excellent, his position regarding the socialist countries in Latin America and our own national security is right on target, and he calls a spade a spade. The USA will not survive on compassion alone, someone has to make the tough decisions. The president has placed excellent leaders around him, General Mattis, John Bolton, Mike Pompeo, Nikki Haley just to name a few, who are very knowledgeable in their fields and are moving our country in the right direction. I would like to see better choices as to environment, health care and education, but can't have it all, and 8 years of Obama, put us in a very weak and dangerous position in the foreign policy arena. I have a hard time with the focus, being the president. Not only because it contributes to the divide, but also because I wish to respect the Office of the President and the person who occupies that office. I would much rather discuss specific behaviors without saying who does it and even without labeling them. When we can describe behavior and discuss actions and how they impact us, we take our eyes off everyone else and we place them back on us. As we see more of what we like and don't like of each specific action/ behavior, we can take steps to avoid them, reject them and embrace positive actions to counter those attitudes in our own lives, as well as community. That in turn, will spill into the national arena.

Love you Diane! You have much courage to invite us into this dialogue.

Diane Altomare: Claire, I so agree with you when you say, that we have to place the focus on ourselves individually. But when we don't call out the unacceptable behavior of the president, we allow it to be the elephant in the room that's not being addressed and I believe it is infecting the country. As a leader, he is a model for others. Although this is not an easy conversation to have, it is essential.

Claire: Diane Altomare -you know, my maternal grandfather was a lot like President Trump, all the negatives...but he was also a very pragmatic leader with incredible courage to stand alone if need be and do what was needed, to protect his family. I have spent my life "calling him out on things." We were close, but conflict reigned in our relationship.

As I am now in my 60's, I don't feel the need to call people out on their negatives, just protect my children and grandchildren from it, but knowing that a time comes when detachment from the person or the behavior is the most conducive to peace. In the case of a president, we will always have those who like the president and those who don't. When we don't, we respect the office and the majority who elected him, and work to prepare an alternative opposition candidate on the next election. Attacking him is not my option.

Diane Altomare: Claire, so beautifully said and I am not attacking the president either. I am declaring that I do not stand in alignment with his consistent labeling and name calling and it's not OK with me, regardless of his policies. I can express how I feel without attacking.

Andrea: Diane, I totally agree with you. There is such a thing as doing a job...and how you do the job. There are lies and drama everyday. This person in the white house doesn't know what integrity is. He is a liar and changes his opinions constantly. If he was a child in school getting good grades but cheating and bullying we wouldn't approve or support it. He is ignorant, unkind and classless. Welcome to America. What a disgrace he is. It certainly speaks of what kind of people we have become that this man represents our country. The rest of the world laughs at him.

Diane Altomare: Yes and thank you for sharing that Andrea...that was so eloquently said! So many overlook his disgraceful behavior because he is benefiting them in some way or they feel that more jobs justifies being mean, unkind and bullying other people. It just isn't OK and this kind of leadership does not represent who I am and what America stands for. And we must continue to voice how we feel, even though it may be difficult for people who support his policies, to hear.

Nicole: Just as athletic stars get "called out" on their behavior, because people want to see them as a role model...I think it is within our rights to ask the president to act more respectful...PRESIDENTIAL.

Mark: I agree Nicole, sadly politicians act like they are in Jr. High. Like Andrea, are we married because my wife thinks the same thing as you, yet she does not use those words around me or likewise, I would use on Obama, Clinton, Mueller, Comey, Pelosi and on and on...because I call her those names every time I vent, not healthy. I believe, Diane correct me if I'm wrong, is trying to bridge a divide when friends and family divide. Diane is trying to bridge the pain that is obvious here, mine is the constant attack on my president that even pushes me out of this post, yet I see Diane and I are friends, with different views. If you see, I don't name call but I feel, the Democratic leadership you have to offer the 63 million, is twice as bad in their illegal schemes, even worse than Trump's behaviors. Peace amongst the chaos! I like this 12 step verse: God, grant me the serenity to accept the things I cannot change, the courage to change the things I can, and wisdom to know the difference.

Beth: I don't agree with some of the things he says but I do believe that he is doing more of what he said he was going to do, than some of our other presidents, in the short time he has been in the position. The other party is constantly berating him and looking for more and more to punish. He is on the defensive for good reason. He constantly has to prove himself, when in fact he is trying to do what he said he would do for us. I still like him and I wish people would let the crap stop. What happened before in his marriage should be between him and his wife. They need to stop digging up junk and let him try to get the job done, he is our president, he was elected.

Andrea: Beth, it is impossible to not call out his lies and his racism. Regarding your remark about people caring about his affairs before he was married...first of all, he has cheated on every wife he has had, including this one. What people are discussing is that he lied and had his lawyer pay her off and perhaps from campaign funds. We wish this is the worst of his behavior and choices, but it is not. There have been too many to mention but the latest being his canceling talks with North Korea. He has no experience or intellect for the job.

Diane Altomare: Andrea yes, we must call out his lies, his racism, his name calling or whatever we are each seeing that is not acceptable and doesn't represent our values or the values of our country.

Everyone is entitled to their opinion, how they feel, what they view is important and how to solve the many issues we are facing. Many have shared their cynicism about healing the emotional divide and have declared that there is no way we can come together again, after all that has taken place.

While I understand this viewpoint and have felt it at times myself, I have seen this work change people. People that were brazen, intensely heated, painstakingly critical or just outright mean to others, have softened. In addition, I've seen many people's hot buttons diminish and people embrace their projections, acknowledging how their jabs or insults weren't effective and a result of their anger and upset.

I've also witnessed many people who have been made wrong for their view, learn how to process that criticism in a healthy way and respond in a loving, civil way, instead of attacking back with name calling or insults. Because of all that I've witnessed from this vantage point, I believe wholeheartedly that people do want to work through this. From a deep place, most of us want to heal this division. And whenever I start to feel cynical or futile about what's happening in our country, I remind myself of this very truth.

HEALING THE EMOTIONAL DIVIDE

The mission of healing the emotional divide is simply to have conversations with people that are based in kindness, respect and compassion, as well as listening to how others feel, without attacking, belittling or name calling.

Very simply, to be able to have civil, kind, loving conversations with people that disagree with you.

Why is this so important? Because many people have a relationship in their life that is being destroyed by this political division, and our emotional well-being and democracy depends on this very healing.

We are each other's, best teachers. And if we lead by example and require that other people are kind, civil and loving when they communicate with us, we will begin to bridge the gap by opening up civil discussions and no longer allowing attacking, insulting, belittling or labeling, in any conversation we have.

The work of healing the emotional divide is simple, although it certainly isn't always easy to do.

THE CHALLENGE

Start now. Simply make a commitment to weave one or two of these into your conversations this week.

1. Have conversations with people that disagree with you politically, from a place of love, respect and compassion.
2. Tone down the intense language. Leave out the jabs or the insults.
3. Process through your emotions and embrace your shadows. When needed, refer back to chapters two and seven.
4. Be intentional about the energy you're infusing in your conversations. Use the

232

visual in chapter eight to decide what you
want to bring more of into your dialogue.
Remembering, that what touches the
other person, also touches you. Realizing
that what you put in the circle between
the two of you, will eventually come back
to you.

ONE HEART CONNECTION

Reconnecting to each other one heart connection
and one conversation at a time, is the work of healing the emotional divide. It's not always easy to do,
but our democracy and the emotional well-being of
our country depends on us, bridging this gap.

I will always stand by what I shared early on in
healing the emotional divide:

*It simply doesn't matter to me where you stand polit-
ically, what side you are on or why.*

*I will never unfriend or unfollow you or stop talk-
ing to you at a dinner party because of your political
views.*

*I see way beyond the smallness of our differences
and honor you as a whole complex human being,
instead of judging you as someone, who either politically agrees or disagrees with me.*

We, as a country, have created this mess together and together, we must clean it up.

One conversation. And one heart connection at a time.

Will you stand with me in this mission? Love, Diane #healtheemotionaldivide

Resources

The Ford Institute, was created by Debbie Ford, an expert in the field of personal transformation, best known for her groundbreaking work on the shadow. Debbie's book that forever changed my life and one that I am eternally grateful for is, *The Dark Side of the Light Chasers.* She also created The Shadow Process Workshop, a three day, heart-opening experience that will teach you how to love yourself unconditionally and will forever, change how you feel about yourself and your life: www.thefordinstitute.com/shadowprocess

The Clarity Book Club series, a ten week tele-series, will support you in transcending your limitations while guiding you to gain clarity, as you create more love, abundance and success in your life: www.dianealtomare.com/claritybookclub

ACKNOWLEDGMENTS

This has been quite a journey. I am forever grateful to everyone who has not only supported me throughout the writing of this book, but to the many of you that contributed your thoughts, your views and your heart, as well. Words can't express the immense gratitude I feel for our connection and our collective choice, to continually dream of, envision and create a better country and world, for ourselves and future generations to come.

To Arielle Ford and Brian Hilliard, for your dear friendship, love and for always being a soft place to land.

To Debbie Ford, your brilliance lives on. Thank you for entrusting me with your profound work, and the enriching and humbling experience of helping people heal and embrace their shadows. I miss you.

To Donna Lipman and Kathy Hertz, soul sisters in bringing light to the darkness. Your support and love, means the world to me.

To my friends, Staci Joy, Linda Yeazel, Thomas

Kevin Dolan, Debora Bradley and Linda Keller for urging me to keep on even in the toughest moments, thank you for sharing your heart and your love.

To Angel Reyes and Kirk Kranzer for exemplifying courageous action and modeling the true meaning of speaking out and standing up for what you believe in. You are both truly inspiring.

To every one of my clients, for sharing your dreams, your struggles and your greatness with me, over the past 18 years. I am forever enriched, as a result of working with you.

To Stacey Crnich, my dear friend and photographer, for your uniqueness and for all the moments you brilliantly morphed into anything I needed. You simply rock.

To Danielle and Michael Guren, my dearest friends, I cherish you and your friendship, more than words can express.

To my Mom, Dad, and Sister. I love you.

To my husband and best friend, Christopher, for your never ending support and love, no matter where this topsy-turvy journey of life, has taken us. And to Alexandra, my sweet baby girl, I'm so proud of you and am grateful to be your momma. I'm the luckiest girl to be both of yours. You have my heart.

NOTES

CHAPTER ONE: THE DIVIDE

Here's what some said: Diane Altomare, Facebook, May 20, 2018, https://www.facebook.com/dianealtomare/posts/10156446289538307

My thoughts on Day 28: Diane Altomare, Facebook, April 30, 2018, https://www.facebook.com/dianealtomare/posts/10156398680058307

1st social media thread: Diane Altomare, Facebook, May 30, 2018, https://www.facebook.com/dianealtomare/posts/10156468946808307

2nd social media thread: Diane Altomare, Facebook, May 19, 2018, https://www.facebook.com/dianealtomare/videos/10156443945748307/

3rd social media thread: Diane Altomare, Facebook, May 19, 2018, https://www.facebook.com/dianealtomare/videos/10156443945748307/

Dyer goes on to say: Dr. Wayne W. Dyer, "Why the Inside Matters," Wayne's Blog, June 15, 2013, https://www.drwaynedyer.com/blog/why-the-inside-matters/.

In one of his many incendiary tweets: Donald J. Trump, Twitter, October 31, 2015, https://twitter.com/realdonaldtrump/status/660460909761069057.

The tweets and comments are many: Donald J. Trump, Twitter, December 11, 2017, https://twitter.com/realdonaldtrump/status/660460909761069057.

Said at a campaign rally in Virginia: Alayna Treene, "Why Trump keeps calling Elizabeth Warren Pocahontas," Axios, November 27, 2017, https://www.axios.com/why-trump-keeps-calling-elizabeth-warren-pocahontas-1513307195-dfbd4f53-fd10-4480-be25-1471ed199e4e.html.

The president is attacking Morning Joe co-host Mika Brzezinski and Joe Scarborough: Donald J. Trump, Twitter, June 29, 2017, https://twitter.com/realdonaldtrump/status/880408582310776832, https://twitter.com/realDonaldTrump/status/880410114456465411.

The president aimed at Senator Gillibrand: Donald J. Trump, Twitter, December 12, 2017, https://twitter.com/realDonaldTrump/status/940567812053053441.

CHAPTER TWO: TRANSFORMING ANGER

News flash, Mr. President: Diane Altomare, Facebook, July 6, 2018, https://www.facebook.com/dianealtomare/posts/10156560650268307

Not pit one side against the other: Chris Cillizza, "The 11 most dangerous things Donald Trump said in his Montana speech," CNN, July 6, 2018, https://www.cnn.com/2018/07/06/politics/donald-trump-montana-speech/index.html.

As Debbie Ford, groundbreaking leader on the shadow taught: Debbie Ford, "What Is the

Shadow?" Oprah, April 18, 2010, http://www.oprah.com/spirit/what-is-the-shadow/all.

He has called people he doesn't like: Jasmine C. Lee, Kevin Quealy, "The 487 People, Places and Things Donald Trump Has Insulted on Twitter: A Complete List," The New York Times, July 10, 2018, https://www.nytimes.com/interactive/2016/01/28/upshot/donald-trump-twitter-insults.html.

Debbie Ford, The Dark Side of The Light Chasers (Riverhead Books , 2010), pg. 2.

CHAPTER THREE: RELINQUISHING ANXIETY

Here are a few examples: Donald J. Trump, Twitter, August 1, 2018, https://twitter.com/realdonaldtrump/status/1024646945640525826.

A few examples of the president: Donald J. Trump, Twitter, August 19, 2018, https://twitter.com/realdonaldtrump/status/1031150465759633408.

Talking to the American people through his tweets: Donald J. Trump, Twitter, August 3, 2018, https://twitter.com/realdonaldtrump/status/1025586524782559232.

Trump's aggressive comments and personal attacks at one of his rallies: David Jackson, "Former Intel chief James Clapper on Trump speech: I just find this extremely disturbing," USA Today, August 23, 2017, https://www.usatoday.com/story/news/politics/2017/08/23/former-intel-chief-james-clapper-trump-speech-i-just-find-extremely-disturbing/592817001/.

Social media thread: Diane Altomare, Facebook, July 6, 2018, https://www.facebook.com/dianealtomare/posts/10156560650268307

Trump has tweeted: Donald J. Trump, Twitter, January 2, 2018, https://twitter.com/realdonaldtrump/status/948355557022420992.

Here are a few of the mirage of tweeets: Donald J. Trump, Twitter, August 5, 2018, https://twitter.com/realdonaldtrump/status/1026069857589227520.

Working overtime: Donald J. Trump, Twitter, May 9, 2018, https://twitter.com/realdonaldtrump/status/994179864436596736.

Too bad a large portion: Donald J. Trump, Twitter, August 5, 2018, https://twitter.com/realdonaldtrump/status/1026087766071947265.

The news media is: Donald J. Trump, Twitter, August 16, 2018, https://twitter.com/realdonaldtrump/status/1030074380397752320.

The "fake news" 320 times: Chris Cillizza, "Donald Trump just accidentally revealed something very important about his 'fake news' attacks," CNN, May 9, 2018, https://www.cnn.com/2018/05/09/politics/donald-trump-media-tweet/index.html.

CHAPTER FOUR: TRANSCENDING FEAR

Before he was president: Bob Woodward, Robert Costa, "Transcript: Donald Trump interview with Bob Woodward and Robert Costa," The Washington Post, April 2, 2016, https://www.washingtonpost.com/news/post-politics/wp/2016/04/02/transcript-donald-trump-interview-with-bob-woodward-and-robert-costa/.

Leadership when he said: John Aloysius Farrell, The Operatic Life of Richard Nixon, The Atlantic, January 9, 2013, https://www.theatlantic.com/politics/archive/2013/01/the-operatic-life-of-richard-nixon/266963/.

Social media thread: Diane Altomare, Facebook, July 6, 2018, https://www.facebook.com/dianealtomare/posts/10156560650268307

Trump tweeted: Donald J. Trump, Twitter, July 15, 2018, https://twitter.com/realdonaldtrump/status/1018738368753078273

Social media thread: Diane Altomare, Facebook, July 16, https://www.facebook.com/dianealtomare/posts/10156584218073307

Social media thread: Diane Altomare, Facebook, July 6, 2018, https://www.facebook.com/dianealtomare/posts/10156560650268307

CHAPTER FIVE: OVERCOMING POWERLESSNESS

As President of the United States: Deena Shanker, "Americans Are Officially Freaking Out," Bloomberg, November 1, 2017, https://www.bloomberg.com/news/articles/ 2017-11-01/americans-are-officially-freaking-out.

Dr. Deepak Chopra says: Dr. Deepak Chopra, "America's Shadow: The Real Secret of Donald J. Trump," SF Gate, February 15, 2017, https://www.sfgate.com/opinion/chopra/article/ America-s-Shadow-The-Real-Secret-of-Donald-J-7965248.php.

My post: Diane Altomare, Facebook, June 29, https://www.facebook.com/dianealtomare/ posts/10156543076838307

What am I missing here: Sarah Sanders, Twitter, June 28, 2017, https://twitter.com/presssec/ status/1012469065661763584

Steve Schmidt said on Bill Maher: Transcript, "Real Time with Bill Maher (August 3, 2018) – Full Transcript," Scraps From The Loft, https://scrapsfromtheloft.com/2018/08/05/real-

time-with-bill-maher-august-3-2018-full-tran-
script/.

CHAPTER SIX: REGAINING POWER

Intelligence Community has unanimously
stated: Bob Fredericks, " Russia is continuing
efforts to interfere in US politics: intel chief,"
New York Post, August 2, 2018,
https://nypost.com/2018/08/02/russia-is-contin-
uing-efforts-to-interfere-in-us-politics-intel-
chief/.

Dan Coates stated: Transcript, "Trump Down-
plays Russia Threat After Intelligence Chiefs
Send Warnings to Public," CNN, August 3, 2018,
http://www.cnn.com/TRANSCRIPTS/1808/03/
nday.01.html.

Social media thread: Diane Altomare, Facebook, July 16, https://www.facebook.com/
dianealtomare/posts/10156584218073307

My post: Diane Altomare, Facebook, June 27,
https://www.facebook.com/dianealtomare/
posts/10156538274848307

Prevailed in our country: Doug Stanglin, "Immigrant children: Federal judge orders families separated at border be reunited within 30 days," USA Today, June 27, 2018, https://www.usatoday.com/story/news/politics/2018/06/27/judge-orders-families-separated-border-reunited-within-30-days/737194002/.

CHAPTER SEVEN: REACTIVATING COURAGE

My post: Diane Altomare, Facebook, August 11, https://www.facebook.com/dianealtomare/posts/10156647364048307

The nightmare of the Trump administration's: Kirsten Gillibrand, Twitter, August 11, 2018, https://twitter.com/SenGillibrand/status/1028282525880381440.

Here's what I shared: Diane Altomare, Facebook, June 28, https://www.facebook.com/dianealtomare/posts/10156540481958307

Dyer said: Dr. Wayne W. Dyer, "Why the Inside Matters," Wayne's Blog, June 15, 2013, https://www.drwaynedyer.com/blog/why-the-inside-matters/.

Debbie Ford, The Dark Side of The Light Chasers (Riverhead Books , 2010), pg. 11.

One was in response to a reporter: Toi Staff, Agencies,"Trump once again proclaims himself a very stable genius," The Times of Isreal, July 12, 2018, https://www.timesofisrael.com/trump-once-again-proclaims-himself-a-very-stable-genius/.

The president in a bad light: Donald J. Trump, Twitter, January 6, 2018, https://twitter.com/realdonaldtrump/status/949618475877765120, https://twitter.com/realdonaldtrump/status/949619270631256064.

As of this writing: Jasmine C. Lee, Kevin Quealy, "The 487 People, Places and Things Donald
Trump Has Insulted on Twitter: A Complete List," The New York Times, July 10, 2018, https://www.nytimes.com/interactive/2016/01/28/upshot/donald-trump-twitter-insults.html.

CHAPTER EIGHT: RESPONDING PEACEFULLY

My post: Diane Altomare, Facebook, June 25, https://www.facebook.com/dianealtomare/posts/10156533556058307

Thank you Jacob Soboroff: Jacob Soboroff, Twitter, June 25, 2018, https://twitter.com/jacobsoboroff/status/1011268424129961985.

My post: Diane Altomare, Facebook, June 29, https://www.facebook.com/dianealtomare/posts/10156542906443307

Brian Karem: Transcript, "Gunman Kills 5 at Maryland Newspaper," CNN, June 29, 2018, http://transcripts.cnn.com/TRANSCRIPTS/1806/29/nday.01.html.

My post: Diane Altomare, Facebook, June 19, https://www.facebook.com/dianealtomare/posts/10156519487703307

CHAPTER NINE: FORGING AHEAD POWERFULLY

The Fake News hates me saying: Donald J. Trump, Twitter, August 5, 2018, https://twitter.com/realdonaldtrump/status/ 1026069857589227520.

Just remember: Rob Tornoe, "Trump to veterans: Don't believe what you're reading or seeing," *The Inquirer*, July 24, 2018, http://www2.philly.com/philly/news/politics/presidential/donald-trump-vfw-speech-kansas-city-what-youre-seeing-reading-not-whats-happening-20180724.html.

So funny to watch: Donald J. Trump, Twitter, June 13, 2018, https://twitter.com/realdonaldtrump/status/1006891643985854464

John Avlon said: Transcript, "White House 'Can't Guarantee' Trump Hasn't Used the 'N'-Word," CNN, August 15, 2018, http://transcripts.cnn.com/TRANSCRIPTS/1808/15/nday.01.html.

Carl Bernstein said: Transcript, "Trump Revokes Ex-CIA Director John Brennan's Security Clearance," CNN, August 15, 2018, http://transcripts.cnn.com/TRANSCRIPTS/1808/15/acd.01.html.

Jim Acosta tweeted: Jim Acosta, Twitter, June 12, 2018, https://twitter.com/acosta/status/1006696409859411968.

Lesley Stahl recalls: Dan Mangan, "President Trump told Lesley Stahl he bashes press 'to demean you and discredit you so ... no one will believe' negative stories about him," CNBC, May 22, 2018, https://www.cnbc.com/2018/05/22/trump-told-lesley-stahl-he-bashes-press-to-discredit-negative-stories.html.

David Gergen said: Transcript, "Trump Revokes Ex-CIA Director John Brennan's Security Clearance," CNN, August 15, 2018, http://transcripts.cnn.com/TRANSCRIPTS/1808/15/acd.01.html.

Brian Stelter said: Transcript, "President Trump Upset About Negative Summit Coverage," CNN, June 13, 2018, http://transcripts.cnn.com/TRANSCRIPTS/1806/13/sitroom.02.html.

Dan Rather tweeted: Dan Rather, Twitter, August 1, 2018, https://twitter.com/danrather/status/1024819108502757376.

General Michael Hayden said: Transcript, "Trump Revokes Ex-CIA Director John Brennan's Security Clearance," CNN, August 15, 2018, http://transcripts.cnn.com/TRANSCRIPTS/1808/15/acd.01.html.

This statement signed: Maegan Vazquez, "175 former US officials added to list denouncing Trump for revoking Brennan's security clearance," CNN, August 20, 2018, https://www.cnn.com/2018/08/20/politics/john-brennan-more-intelligence-officials-statement/index.html.

Here's a quote: Mahita Gajanan, "What You're Seeing... Is Not What's Happening. People Are Comparing This Trump Quote to George Orwell," Time, July 24, 2018, http://time.com/5347737/trump-quote-george-orwell-vfw-speech/.

As Theodore Roosevelt stated: Lily Rothman, "The Story Behind Jeff Flake's Teddy Roosevelt Quote on Why Criticizing the President Matters," Time, October 24, 2017, http://time.com/

4995774/jeff-flake-teddy-roosevelt-quote-donald-trump/.

My post: Diane Altomare, Facebook, June 30, https://www.facebook.com/dianealtomare/posts/10156545204943307

CHAPTER TEN: THE RECONNECT

Lincoln: Neely, Mark E. Jr, 1982, *The Abraham Lincoln Encyclopedia*, (New York: Da Capo Press, Inc.)

My post: Diane Altomare, Facebook, May 15, https://www.facebook.com/dianealtomare/posts/10156435633898307

ABOUT THE AUTHOR

Diane Altomare is a certified integrative master coach to thousands of people worldwide, the author of *Clarity: 10 Proven Strategies to Transform Your Life* and the executive producer and host of Politically Emotional radio.

As an emotional expert, she is often featured on NBC, ABC7 Eyewitness News, as well as CBS Radio and NPR and has contributed to many publications including Mind Body Green, AARP and the Chicago Tribune.

For the past 17 years, as a beloved motivational speaker and workshop leader, she has helped thousands of people transform from a limiting past to an inspiring future. Known as "the coach with the authentic, gentle & laser-focused approach," she has a gift for nailing the deep truth behind any situation.

Connect with Diane on Facebook at www.facebook.com/Diane.Altomare or on Twitter at www.twitter.com/DianeAltomare.

To learn more, visit
www.DianeAltomare.com

CPSIA information can be obtained
at www.ICGtesting.com
Printed in the USA
LVHW111606291118
598661LV00005B/784/P